Process Costing

E Harris

Viva Books Private Limited
New Delhi • Mumbai • Chennai • Kolkata

First South Asian Edition 2002

VIVA BOOKS PRIVATE LIMITED

- 4262/3 Ansari Road, Daryaganj, New Delhi 110 002
  e-mail : viva@mantraonline.com
- 214 New Apollo Industrial Estate, 2nd Floor, Mogra Lane, Andheri (E), Mumbai 400 069
  e-mail : vivabooks@mantraonline.com
- 7 Aziz Mulk, Seventh Street, Thousand Lights, Chennai 600 006
  e-mail : vivachennai@mantraonline.com
- 6-A, Rifle Range Road, Kolkata 700 019
  e-mail : vivakolkata@mantraonline.com

Visit us at **www.vivagroupindia.com**

Published by Arrangement with
The Chartered Institute of Management Accountants
26 Chapter Street
London SW1P 4NP
UK.

ISBN : 81-7649-317-1

Rs. 100

Published by Vinod Vasishtha for Viva Books Private Limited,
4262/3 Ansari Road, Daryaganj, New Delhi 110 002
Printed at Raj Press, R-3 Inderpuri, New Delhi - 110012

Contents

CHAPTER 1

Introduction ... 1

Different methods of costing ... 2

CHAPTER 2

Continuous operation/process costing – normal and abnormal losses, abnormal gains ... 3

Average costing ... 3

Simple process accounts ... 4

Process accounts with normal losses ... 6

Process accounts with abnormal losses ... 9

Process accounts with abnormal gains ... 12

Accounting for normal and abnormal losses, and abnormal gains ... 15

Summary of the rules ... 19

CHAPTER 3

Continuous operation/process costing – work in progress ... 21

Introduction ... 21

The concept of equivalent units ... 21

Work in progress at different stages of completion ... 24

Opening work in progress ... 26

Opening work in progress – FIFO method ... 26

Opening work in progress – average method ... 31

A previous process ... 33

Equivalent units, normal and abnormal losses ... 36

Losses discovered when only partially complete ... 36

CHAPTER 4
Process costing examples 41

CHAPTER 5
Joint and by-product costing 57
Introduction 57
The apportionment of joint costs for stock valuation purposes 59
The physical measures basis 59
Further processing decisions 65
By-product costing 66
Accounting for by-products 67

CHAPTER 6
Joint product examples 71

Chapter 1

Introduction

This book covers the more complex areas of the costing of processes and operations. It explains how to determine the average cost per unit in process costing in a simple step-by-step approach, starting with normal losses with no scrap value and working through the treatment of scrap values, abnormal losses and gains and the sometimes confusing areas of opening and closing work in progress.

The topic of joint product costing is explained, covering both the different methods which can be used to value stock for determining the profit for the period, and the type of information which is required for a further processing decision.

The book also covers the distinction between joint products and by-products and the accounting treatment required by these types of products.

Questions on one of these costing methods frequently appear in professional examinations at the earlier levels. There has also been a trend to examine students with more complex questions in such areas as process costing and joint product costing, sometimes combined with another topic, for example, variance analysis, at more advanced stages of the professional examinations.

The examples in Chapter 4 should be attempted after working through Chapters 2 and 3, which cover process costing. The examples in Chapter 6 should be attempted after working through Chapter 5 on joint and by-product costing.

There is no point in simply reading through the answers. If you check your answers against those provided, this will help to highlight areas where more practice is needed.

DIFFERENT METHODS OF COSTING

The CIMA *Official Terminology* identifies two basic methods of costing which are used to suit the methods by which goods are manufactured or services are provided:

(a) *specific order costing*, which is 'applicable where work consists of separate contracts, jobs or batches', (CIMA *Terminology*, p. 38);

(b) *continuous operation/process costing*, which is 'applicable where goods or services result from a sequence of continuous or repetitive operations or processes. Costs are averaged over the units produced during the period' (CIMA *Terminology*, p. 38).

These two general terms highlight the two major methods of production. It is not always obvious which method of costing is to be used and it is important for you to identify correctly the appropriate method.

The objectives of this book are to provide:

(a) a thorough understanding of the accounting procedures for continuous operation/process costing, including the treatment of normal and abnormal losses and gains as well as opening and closing work in progress.

(b) an explanation of the different techniques to be used when accounting for joint products and by-products. The distinction between the methods used to value stock for profit determination and the method used for decision-making purposes is clearly explained.

Chapter 2

Continuous Operation/ Process Costing – Normal and Abnormal Losses, Abnormal Gains

AVERAGE COSTING

For the remainder of this text 'continuous operation/process costing' will be referred to as process costing, but the significance of the 'continuous operation' aspect must always be kept well in mind.

Process costing systems are used by the paint, chemical, oil and textile industries. In these mass production industries, it is often difficult to identify an individual cost unit during production and processing, so it is necessary to take a broader view of the situation when establishing a production cost per unit produced.

No attempt is made to identify costs with specific units. Instead, an *average* cost is derived by dividing the total costs for a period of time by the total number of units produced in that period.

The *average* cost per unit is required not only for internal control purposes, but also for the valuation of finished goods and work in progress.

This chapter demonstrates how to arrive at the average cost per unit by using a series of examples which become more complex at each stage.

Major features of process costing

- Finished goods are produced from a system of separate, consecutive processes (sometimes known as departments). Each department performs part of the total operation and each stage of production must be completed before the next stage is started. The accounting procedures follow this pattern and each process or stage will have its details recorded in a process account, the costs being debited and the output from the process being credited. Materials and labour costs will be specifically identified with the process and overhead costs will be absorbed in the same way as in other accounting systems.

- As the output of one process becomes the input of the next process, the cumulative costs are transferred from one process account to the next, until all the stages are completed.

- As output is transferred from one process to the next, a unit cost is calculated. This can be compared with the standard cost of the process or with the cost of the previous period. This will help to inform management of inefficiencies or trends in costs.

- Losses due to evaporation or spoilage may occur in the process. If no loss is expected, then any loss will be abnormal. If a certain level of loss is expected, the actual loss may well exceed this, giving rise to an *abnormal loss*. Alternatively, the actual loss may be less than expected, giving rise to an *abnormal gain*.

  The accounting treatment of normal losses differs from that of abnormal losses and gains. Normal losses are expected to occur during the course of production and their cost is absorbed by the completed output. Abnormal losses and gains are shown separately in the profit and loss account and treated in a similar manner to yield variances.

- The output from the process may be a single product, but there may also be joint products and by-products. The accounting treatment of joint products and by-products is explained in Chapter 5.

SIMPLE PROCESS ACCOUNTS

Process costing usually requires the completion of the process account. This involves the calculation of a cost per unit, possibly for more than one process. This topic can be confusing, but there is no need for this, provided the basic rules or guidelines are followed:

Rule 1

Always draw up a process account for each process. There should be columns for the 'quantities' accounted for, as well as for the costs (and revenues). The 'quantities' may be the units, kilograms or litres of *input* which must be entered on the debit side and accounted for as *output* on the credit side.

Rule 2

Enter the data into the process account and make sure that the 'units' columns are balanced before attempting to calculate the cost per unit.

Rule 3

The cost per unit (CPU) is based on *everything that is normal.* The importance of this will become evident later in this chapter when dealing with the accounting treatment of losses.

Example 1 Simple process account

Lowd is produced from a single process. The inputs for the month are as follows:

	kg	£
Materials	1,000	1,000
Labour		2,000
Overhead absorbed		2,000

Output was 1,000kg and there are no process losses.

Prepare the account for the process.

Answer and explanation

Rules 1 and 2: draw up the process account, enter the data and make sure that the 'units' columns are balanced.

Process account

	kg	£		*kg*	£
Materials	1,000	1,000	Output	1,000	
Labour		2,000			
Overhead		2,000			

When it is shown that the units columns are balanced, then it is safe to proceed with the calculation of the cost per unit.

Rule 3: the cost per unit is based on everything that is *normal.* In this example, it is only necessary to take into account the input costs, and the output (which is as expected, or normal).

$$\text{Cost per unit} = \frac{\text{Input costs}}{\text{Normal output}}$$

$$= \frac{£1{,}000 + £2{,}000 + £2{,}000}{1{,}000\text{kg}} = \frac{£5{,}000}{1{,}000\text{kg}} = £5 \text{ per kg}$$

The output in the process account can now be valued at £5 per kg and the account can be completed.

It is extremely helpful to have a specific column to show the cost per unit (CPU) on the credit side of the process account, and this approach will be followed. The process account will now be shown as:

Process account

	kg	*£*		*kg*	*CPU*	*£*
Materials	1,000	1,000	Output	1,000	£5	5,000
Labour		2,000				
Overhead		2,000				
	1,000	5,000		1,000		5,000

PROCESS ACCOUNTS WITH NORMAL LOSSES

It is common to find that the output from the process is less than the total input. This may be due to evaporation of liquids, or scrap resulting from the high-quality output required. Where the loss is unavoidable, an average level of loss is determined and this is known as the *normal loss*. It is often expressed as a percentage of the total input.

Losses may or may not have a scrap value. If the loss is caused by evaporation, there will be no scrap value, but if the loss is caused by defective units it is likely that there will be a potential scrap value.

The normal loss must always be accounted for in the process account in the 'units' column, but the only value ever assigned to a normal loss is its scrap value. If it has no scrap value, it has no value to be accounted for.

Example 2 Normal loss, no scrap value

The inputs to a process in November were as follows:

	kg	£
Materials	1,000	1,000
Labour		2,000
Overhead absorbed		1,500

Output was 900 units. The normal loss rate is 10% of the input. The loss has no scrap value.

Prepare the account for the process.

Answer and explanation

Remember that you will gain the greatest benefit from these examples if you draw up an outline process account and enter the relevant data from the example.

Rules 1, 2 and 3:

Process account

	kg	£		*kg*	*CPU*	£
Materials	1,000	1,000	Normal loss	100	–	–
Labour		2,000	Output	900	£5	4,500
Overhead		1,500				
	1,000	4,500		1,000		4,500

Notes

1 The normal loss is included on the credit side to help to account for the input. As it does not have a scrap value, no value is assigned to it (show this by entering dashes in the money column as shown).

2 The cost per unit is based on everything that is normal, i.e.

$$\text{CPU} = \frac{\text{Normal costs}}{\text{Normal output}}$$

$$= \frac{£1{,}000 + £2{,}000 + £2{,}000}{900\text{kg}} = £5 \text{ per kg}$$

3 Note that the *normal* output is determined by subtracting the normal loss from the actual input, i.e., 1,000kg – 100kg = 900kg normal output.

Rule 4
The only value ever assigned to a normal loss is its scrap value. If there is no scrap value then there is no value to account for.

Example 3 Normal loss with a scrap value
The inputs to a process in December were as follows:

	kg	*£*
Materials	1,000	1,000
Labour		2,000
Overhead absorbed		1,700

Output was 900 units. The normal loss rate is 10% of the input. Scrapped units can be sold for £2 per kg.

Prepare the account for the process.

Answer and explanation
First draw up the process account and include all the relevant information.

Process account

	kg	*£*		*kg*	*CPU*	*£*
Materials	1,000	1,000	Normal loss	100	£2	200
Labour		2,000	Output	900		
Overhead		1,700				

When the process account is drawn up in this way, it shows two important features:

(a) The 'units' columns balance as shown. This is vital before proceeding with the calculation of the cost per unit.
(b) The scrap value of the normal loss is credited to the cost of production, and is therefore used to reduce the overall cost. This could perhaps be shown more clearly by entering the scrap value as a minus item on the debit side, but the principles of double entry require it to be shown on the credit side.

The next step is to value the cost per unit. This is again based on everything that is *normal*, i.e., normal costs, normal scrap proceeds and normal output.

$$\text{CPU} = \frac{\text{Normal costs less normal scrap proceeds}}{\text{Normal output}}$$

$$= \frac{£4{,}700 - £200}{900\text{kg}} = £5 \text{ per kg}$$

Finally, show this in the process account:

Process account

	kg	*£*		*kg*	*CPU*	*£*
Materials	1,000	1,000	Normal loss	100	£2	200
Labour		2,000	Output	900	£5	4,500
Overhead		1,700				
	1,000	4,700		1,000		4,700

PROCESS ACCOUNTS WITH ABNORMAL LOSSES

An abnormal loss will arise where the actual loss is greater than expected. It may be that no loss is expected, in which case any loss will be abnormal. Suppose, for example, that the input to the process is 10,000 units with a normal loss rate of 10% of the input, but the actual ouput is 8,500 units. In this case, there will still be a normal loss of 1,000 units, which is accounted for in the usual way (depending on whether or not it has a scrap value). In addition there will be an abnormal loss of 500 units, which must also be accounted for.

Rule 5
Abnormal losses and gains are valued at the normal cost per unit in the process account.

This might sound a contradiction in terms, but abnormal losses and gains are valued at the same cost per unit as the good output, which enables the effect of these unexpected differences to be properly identified in the management accounts for control purposes. In some ways, this makes the accounting more simple. The accounting treatment ensures that abnormal losses are charged to the period in which they are incurred and cannot be carried forward to a future period in the stock valuation.

Example 4 Normal and abnormal losses, no scrap value

The inputs to a process in January were as follows:

	kg	*£*
Materials	1,000	2,000
Labour		4,000
Overhead absorbed		3,000

Output was 850kg. The normal loss rate is 10% of the input. The losses have no scrap value.

Prepare the account for the process.

Answer and explanation

First draw up the process account and include all the relevant information.

Process account

	kg	*£*		*kg*	*CPU*	*£*
Materials	1,000	2,000	Normal loss	100	–	–
Labour		4,000	Abnormal loss	50		
Overhead		3,000	Output	850		

The information is entered in the process account as usual. The normal loss of 100kg has no value. The abnormal loss will be valued at the normal cost per unit. As the 'units' column is now shown to balance, the cost per unit can be calculated based on *everything that is normal* – normal costs, normal scrap proceeds (if any) and normal output.

$$\text{CPU} = \frac{\text{Normal costs}}{\text{Normal output}}$$

$$= \frac{£2{,}000 + £4{,}000 + £3{,}000}{900\text{kg}} = £10 \text{ per kg}$$

To complete the process account:

Process account

	kg	*£*		*kg*	*CPU*	*£*
Materials	1,000	2,000	Normal loss	100	–	–
Labour		4,000	Abnormal loss	50	£10	500
Overhead		3,000	Output	850	£10	8,500
	1,000	9,000		1,000		9,000

Notes

1 The abnormal loss is valued at exactly the same cost per unit as the output. This will always be the case in the process account whereby abnormal gains and losses are treated, for control purposes, as the equivalent of the good output in arriving at the cost per unit.

2 The calculation of the cost per unit is based on *everything that is normal*. For this reason the normal output is the basis of the calculation, *never* the actual output.

Example 5 Normal and abnormal losses with a scrap value

The inputs to a process in February were as follows:

	kg	*£*
Materials	1,000	2,000
Labour		4,000
Overhead absorbed		3,400

Output was 820kg. The normal loss rate is 10% of the input. Scrapped units can be sold for £4 per kg.

Prepare the account for the process.

Answer and explanation

First draw up the process account and include all the relevant information.

Process account

	kg	*£*		*kg*	*CPU*	*£*
Materials	1,000	2,000	Normal loss	100	£4	400
Labour		4,000	Abnormal loss	80		
Overhead		3,400	Output	820		

The information is entered as usual. The normal loss has a scrap value of £4 per kg, which reduces the overall cost of production. Although the abnormal loss of 80kg will also have a scrap value of £4 per kg, only the scrap value from the normal loss is entered at this stage. Remember that the abnormal loss will be stated at the normal cost per unit in the process account.

As the 'units' column is now shown to balance, the cost per unit can be calculated, based on *everything that is normal* – normal costs, normal scrap proceeds and normal output.

$$\text{CPU} = \frac{\text{Normal costs less normal scrap proceeds}}{\text{Normal output}}$$

$$= \frac{£2{,}000 + £4{,}000 + £3{,}400 - £400}{900\text{kg}} = £10 \text{ per kg}$$

To complete the process account:

Process account

	kg	*£*		*kg*	*CPU*	*£*
Materials	1,000	2,000	Normal loss	100	£4	400
Labour		4,000	Abnormal loss	80	£10	800
Overhead		3,400	Output	820	£10	8,200
	1,000	9,400		1,000		9,400

PROCESS ACCOUNTS WITH ABNORMAL GAINS

An abnormal gain will arise where the actual loss is less than expected. There should always be a normal loss, which may or may not have a scrap value. Suppose that the input to the process is 10,000 units, the normal loss rate is 10% of the input and the actual output is 9,100 units. There will still be a *normal loss* of 1,000 units, but in this case it will be offset by an abnormal gain of 100 units, as the actual loss is less than expected. Both the normal loss and the abnormal gain must be accounted for.

Example 6 Normal losses, abnormal gains, no scrap value
The inputs to a process in March were as follows:

	kg	*£*
Materials	1,000	1,000
Labour		2,000
Overhead absorbed		1,500

Output was 920kg. The normal loss rate is 10% of the input. The losses have no scrap value.

Prepare the account for the process.

Answer and explanation
First draw up the process account and include all the relevant information.

Process account

	kg	*CPU*	*£*		*kg*	*CPU*	*£*
Materials	1,000		1,000	Normal loss	100	–	–
Labour			2,000	Output	920		
Overhead			1,500				
Abnormal gain	20						

The information is entered in the process account as usual, i.e., the inputs, the normal loss and the actual output. A check on the units column will reveal whether there is an abnormal loss or an abnormal gain. In this example the actual output is 920 units, whereas the expected or normal output is 900 units. It is the *additional* 20 units which give rise to an abnormal gain. In the process account, the abnormal gain is shown on the debit side, which may not at first seem very logical, but it follows the rules of double entry.

As the 'units' column is now shown to balance, the cost per unit can now be calculated based on *everything that is normal* – normal costs, normal scrap (if any) and normal output.

$$\text{CPU} = \frac{\text{Normal costs}}{\text{Normal output}}$$

$$= \frac{£1{,}000 + £2{,}000 + £1{,}500}{900\text{kg}} = \frac{£4{,}500}{900\text{kg}} = £5 \text{ per kg}$$

To complete the process account:

Process account

	kg	*CPU*	*£*		*kg*	*CPU*	*£*
Materials	1,000		1,000	Normal loss	100	–	–
Labour			2,000	Output	920	£5	4,600
Overhead			1,500				
Abnormal gain	20	£5	100				
	1,020		4,600		1,020		4,600

Notes

1 The abnormal gain is valued at exactly the same cost per unit as the output in the process account. This is the same valuation as with normal losses. The principles of valuation are identical – output, abnormal

losses and abnormal gains are valued at the normal cost per unit in the process account.

2 The cost per unit is still based on *everything that is normal*, including normal output.

3 The normal output can also be made up as:
(i) actual output plus abnormal loss;
(ii) actual output less abnormal gain.

Example 7 Normal losses, abnormal gains, scrap values
The inputs to a process in April were as follows:

	kg	*£*
Materials	1,000	1,000
Labour		2,000
Overhead absorbed		1,700

Output was 930kg. The normal loss rate is 10% of the input. Scrapped units can be sold for £2 per kg.

Prepare the account for the process.

Answer and explanation
First draw up the process account and include all the relevant information.

Process account

	kg	*CPU*	*£*		*kg*	*CPU*	*£*
Materials	1,000		1,000	Normal loss	100	£2	£200
Labour			2,000	Output	930		
Overhead			1,700				
Abnormal gain	30						

All the necessary principles have already been explained. This example simply involves a combination of these principles.

When the units column is shown to balance, the cost per unit can be calculated, based on *everything that is normal* including normal output.

$$\text{CPU} = \frac{\text{Normal costs less normal scrap proceeds}}{\text{Normal output}}$$

$$= \frac{£1,000 + £2,000 + £1,700 - £200}{900\text{kg}} = £5 \text{ per kg}$$

The completed process account will then appear as follows:

Process account

	kg	*CPU*	*£*		*kg*	*CPU*	*£*
Materials	1,000		1,000	Normal loss	100	£2	200
Labour			2,000	Output	930	£5	4,650
Overhead			1,700				
Abnormal gain	30	£5	150				
	1,030		4,850		1,030		4,850

Notes

1 It should be remembered that the 'totals' in the process accounts are only to ensure that the account is 'balanced' for double entry purposes and have no other meaning.

2 In the last two examples a CPU column has been shown on the debit side. There should always be a CPU column on the credit side to show the valuation of the normal loss, abnormal loss and the actual output. It is only necessary to have a CPU column on the debit side when there is an abnormal gain.

ACCOUNTING FOR NORMAL AND ABNORMAL LOSSES, AND ABNORMAL GAINS

The text so far has concentrated on the valuation of normal and abnormal losses and abnormal gains in the process account. However, the normal rules of double entry still apply, and normal loss accounts, abnormal loss accounts and abnormal gains accounts are often required.

Referring back to Example 2, Normal loss: no normal loss account is required as there is no value to be accounted for.

In Example 3, Normal loss with a scrap value: the normal loss account should be drawn up as follows:

Normal loss account

	kg	*CPU*	*£*		*kg*	*CPU*	*£*
Process account	100	£2	200				

This completes the double entry accounting for the normal loss, but does not show its final outcome, which is likely to be a cash sale for which the entries are:

Debit Bank
Credit Normal loss account

with the scrap proceeds.

Normal loss account

	kg	*CPU*	*£*		*kg*	*CPU*	*£*
Process Account	100	£2	200	Bank	100	£2	200

In Example 4, Normal and abnormal losses, no scrap value: there is no double entry to complete for the normal loss, but the abnormal loss must be properly accounted for, and the abnormal loss account drawn up as follows:

Abnormal loss account

	kg	*CPU*	*£*		*kg*	*CPU*	*£*
Process Account	50	£10	500				

Again, this completes the double entry for the abnormal loss, but does not show its final outcome. The amount of the abnormal loss should be shown as a separate item in the profit and loss account, drawing to the attention of management for control purposes the fact that an unexpected cost has arisen, i.e.

Debit Profit and loss
Credit Abnormal loss account

Normal loss account

	kg	*CPU*	*£*		*kg*	*CPU*	*£*
Process account	50	£10	500	Profit & loss	50	£10	500

Example 5, Normal and abnormal losses with a scrap value: this will require the preparation of both a normal loss account and an abnormal loss account to complete the double entry from the process account, as follows:

Normal loss account

	kg	*CPU*	*£*		*kg*	*CPU*	*£*
Process Account	100	£4	400				

Abnormal loss account

	kg	*CPU*	*£*		*kg*	*CPU*	*£*
Process Account	80	£10	800				

The final outcome is that there were 180 defective units available to be sold as scrap. 100 of these were expected as a normal loss, and the proceeds from these have already been taken into account when valuing the cost per unit. The remaining 80 defective units were not expected and are therefore considered an abnormal loss. In the process account they were valued at £10 per unit, but the overall cost to the firm will be less, as the 80 defective units can also be sold as scrap for £4 per unit, reducing the overall cost to £6 per unit.

The sale of the scrap will be recorded as:

		£
Debit	Bank (180 units × £4)	720
Credit	Normal loss account (100 units × £4)	400
Credit	Abnormal loss account (80 units × £4)	320

Normal loss account

	kg	*CPU*	*£*		*kg*	*CPU*	*£*
Process Account	100	£4	400	Bank	100	£4	400

Abnormal loss account

	kg	*CPU*	*£*		*kg*	*CPU*	*£*
Process Account	80	£10	800	Bank	80	£4	320
				Profit & loss			480
	80		800		80		800

Note

The charge to the profit and loss account relates to the 80 abnormal loss units. The value is made up as follows:

	£
80 units at cost per unit (£10)	800
Less: scrap value of 80 units (£4)	320
Net cost of abnormal loss (£6 per unit)	480

In Example 6, Normal losses, abnormal gains, no scrap value: the normal loss has no scrap value, so there is no value to be accounted for. The abnormal gain does have a value and this must be accounted for. The abnormal gains account will be drawn up as follows, completing the double entry from the process account:

Abnormal gains account

	kg	*CPU*	*£*		*kg*	*CPU*	*£*
				Process account	20	£5	100

This completes the double entry, but does not show its final outcome. The amount of the abnormal gain should be shown as a separate item in the profit and loss account, drawing the attention of management to the fact that an unexpected benefit has arisen, i.e.

Debit Abnormal gains account
Credit Profit and loss account

Abnormal gains account

	kg	*CPU*	*£*		*kg*	*CPU*	*£*
Profit & loss	20	£5	100	Process account	20	£5	100

Example 7, Normal losses, abnormal gains, scrap values: this will require the preparation of both a normal loss account and an abnormal gains account to complete the double entry from the process account, as follows:

Normal loss account

	kg	*CPU*	*£*		*kg*	*CPU*	*£*
Process ac	100	£2	200				

Abnormal gains account

	kg	*CPU*	*£*		*kg*	*CPU*	*£*
				Process ac	30	£5	150

The final outcome is that there were only 70 defective units available to be sold as scrap, instead of the 100 units expected as a normal loss. However, the proceeds from 100 units of normal loss were taken into account when valuing the cost per unit. The effect of this is that the value of the abnormal gain will not be as great as it at first seems. As output is 30 units greater than expected, the actual scrap sold will be 30 units less than expected, so reducing income by this amount.

The sale of the scrap will be recorded as:

		£
Debit	Bank	140
Credit	Normal loss account (70 units × £2)	140

Then it will be necessary to make a transfer from the normal loss account to the abnormal gains account. The amount of the transfer represents the abnormally gained units at their scrap value – in this example 30 units at £2 per unit. The abnormal gains account can then be closed with a transfer to the credit of the profit and loss account.

Normal loss account

	kg	*CPU*	*£*		*kg*	*CPU*	*£*
Process account	100	£2	200	Bank	70	£2	140
				Abnormal gains (transfer)	30	£2	60
	100		200		100		200

You should remember that the balance on the normal loss account is *never* transferred to the profit and loss account.

Abnormal gains account

	kg	*CPU*	*£*		*kg*	*CPU*	*£*
Normal loss (transfer)	30	£2	60	Process account	30	£5	150
Profit & loss			90				
	30		150		30		150

Note
The credit to the profit and loss account is not just the 'balancing figure' and can be checked as follows:

	£
30 units at cost per unit (£5)	150
Less: scrap value of 30 units (£2) forgone	60
Net amount of abnormal gain (£3 per unit)	90

SUMMARY OF THE RULES

Rule 1
Always draw up the process account with columns for quantities as well as costs (and revenues).

Rule 2

Enter the data in the process account and make sure that the 'units' columns are balanced before attempting to calculate the cost per unit.

Rule 3

The cost per unit is based on *everything that is normal* – normal costs, normal scrap proceeds, normal output. Note that this is the same irrespective of the 'actual' outcome, whether this results in an abnormal loss or an abnormal gain.

Rule 4

The only value ever assigned to a normal loss is its scrap value. If there is no scrap value, then there is no value to account for.

Rule 5

Abnormal losses and gains are valued at the normal cost per unit in the process account.

Rule 6 (mentioned for the first time)

An abnormal loss is seldom as bad as it at first seems and an abnormal gain is seldom as good as it first seems. The reason for this is the effect of the scrap proceeds, which must be taken into account in order to determine the charge or credit to the profit and loss account. This rule will only be true if the normal loss does have a scrap value.

Chapter 3

Continuous Operation/ Process Costing – Work in Progress

INTRODUCTION

The major feature of process costing is that it is used where it is not possible to identify specific cost units arising during the course of production. For this reason the costs incurred are averaged over the units produced in the period.

A second feature is that process costing is used where production is more or less continuous, hence the full title 'continuous operation/process costing'. This gives rise to the problem of valuing work in progress at the end of an accounting period. In practice, there is likely to be work in progress at nearly every stage of production at any time. However, for accounting purposes it is reasonable to take a broader view when establishing a cost per unit and valuing work in progress.

THE CONCEPT OF EQUIVALENT UNITS

At the end of any accounting period, there will be some partly completed units as well as some fully completed units. The input costs will relate to both types of unit. In order to relate these input costs to both of these types of unit, the concept of *equivalent units* is used.

Equivalent units are used to simplify the valuation of partly finished units. The partly finished units are converted into finished unit equivalents for accounting purposes only, in order to determine the unit cost.

For example, assume that at the end of March the total output from the process comprises 9,000 finished units and another 1,000 units which are partly finished. The total costs for the period are £19,000. The partly finished units are considered to be 50% complete and it is assumed that they have incurred only 50% of the cost per unit of the finished units. In order to arrive at a reasonable valuation for the 1,000 partly finished units, they can be converted into equivalent units.

1,000 partly finished units, 50% complete = 500 equivalent units. The total production for the period will comprise (in equivalent units or EU):

		Equivalent Units
Finished units	9,000 × 100%	9,000
Partly finished units	1,000 × 50%	500
Total equivalent units		9,500

As the total costs are £19,000, the cost per unit is determined in the normal way.

$$\text{Cost per equivalent unit} = \frac{\text{Input costs}}{\text{Normal equivalent output}} = \frac{£19{,}000}{9{,}500} = £2 \text{ per equivalent unit}$$

This valuation will apply to both the finished units and the partly finished units.

		£
Finished units 9,000 EU × £2 per unit	=	18,000
Partly finished units 500 EU × £2 per unit	=	1,000
		19,000

However, in reality, there are 1,000 partly finished units, giving each a valuation of £1 each.

Example 8 Simple equivalent units

The inputs to a process in May were as follows:

	Units	£
Materials	1,000	4,000
Labour		2,000
Overhead		3,600

Output was 900 completed units and 100 units which were considered to be 60% complete. Calculate the cost per unit and value the work in progress. Show the process account.

Answer and explanation

The partly completed units can be expressed as 'equivalent units' for costing purposes: 100 units which were 60% complete can be considered to cost the same as 100 × 60%, i.e. 60 completed units. Although not the same in physical terms, it is a very useful costing simplification.

Output can now be expressed as:

	units
Completed units	900
Work in progress: equivalent units	60
Total equivalent units	960

The **cost per unit** can be calculated as:

	£
Costs: Materials	4,000
Labour	2,000
Overhead	3,600
	9,600
Equivalent units	960

Cost per unit: $\frac{£9,600}{960 \text{ units}}$ = £10 per unit

Valuation of work in progress:

60 equivalent units at £10 per unit = £600

The **process account** will be shown as:

Process account

	Units	*£*		*Units*	*CPU*	*£*
Materials	1,000	4,000	Output	900	£10	9,000
Labour		2,000	Closing WIP	100		600
Overhead		3,600				
	1,000	9,600		1,000		9,600

Notes

1 The process account is drawn up in the usual way, with columns for units, £ and CPU. Note that it is the *total* number of units of closing work in progress that must be accounted for in the units column. The equivalent units are only used for the purpose of valuation.

2 There is little point in including a cost per unit relating to the work in progress in the process account, but if this is done, it should be shown as £6 per unit.

WORK IN PROGRESS AT DIFFERENT STAGES OF COMPLETION

In practice, the partly finished units or closing work in progress may have reached different stages of completion. In many cases, materials are added at or near the beginning of the process and may be 100% complete, but the labour and overhead content of the work may only be partly complete. If this occurs and work in progress has reached different stages of completion for each of the elements of cost, it is necessary to evaluate each element of cost separately, according to the number of equivalent units for each cost element.

Example 9 Work in progress at different stages of completion
The inputs to a process in June were as follows:

	Units	£
Materials	1,000	4,500
Labour		2,400
Overhead absorbed		2,790

Output was 900 completed units with 100 units of closing work in progress (CWIP). The work in progress had reached the following stages of completion:

Materials	100%
Labour	60%
Overhead	30%

Complete the process account.

Answer and explanation
Draw up the process account and enter the relevant data, making sure that the units are properly accounted for, as follows:

Process account

	Units	*£*		*Units*	*CPU*	*£*
Materials	1,000	4,500	Output	900		
Labour		2,400	CWIP	100		
Overhead		2,790				

Calculate the number of equivalent units (EU) to be related to each element of cost, remembering the different stages of completion of the closing work in progress.

Material:	Completed units	900
	CWIP 100 units × 100%	100
	Total EU	1,000
Labour:	Completed units	900
	CWIP 100 units × 60%	60
	Total EU	960
Overhead:	Completed units	900
	CWIP 100 units × 30%	30
	Total EU	930

Calculate the cost per unit for each cost element:

Materials $\frac{£4{,}500}{1{,}000\text{ EU}} = £4.50$ per EU

Labour $\frac{£2{,}400}{960\text{ EU}} = £2.50$ per EU

Overhead $\frac{£2{,}790}{930\text{ EU}} = £3.00$ per EU

A completed unit is valued at the sum of these, i.e. £4.50 + £2.50 + £3.00 = £10.

The work in progress is valued as:

		£
Materials	100 EU × £4.50	450
Labour	60 EU × £2.50	150
Overhead	30 EU × £3.00	90
Work in progress		690

Finally, complete the process account:

Process account

	Units	*£*		*Units*	*CPU*	*£*
Materials	1,000	4,500	Output	900	£10	9,000
Labour		2,400	CWIP	100		690
Overhead		2,790				
	1,000	9,690		1,000		9,690

Note: the closing work in progress can be shown at a cost of £6.90 per unit.

OPENING WORK IN PROGRESS

It follows that if there is closing work in progress at the end of one accounting period, there will be opening work in progress at the start of the next accounting period, which only needs to be finished in order to be converted into completed units.

There are two common assumptions regarding the opening work in progress.

The first, known as the **FIFO method** (first in first out), assumes that the opening work in progress will be processed and completed during the current month.

The second, known as the **average** or **weighted average method**, assumes that the opening work in progress is completely merged with the input from the current month and will not necessarily be completed as part of the current month's output.

OPENING WORK IN PROGRESS – FIFO METHOD

If the FIFO method is used, the percentage degree of completion of each element of the opening work in progress (OWIP) must be given. The cost relating to each element of OWIP is not usually given, but the total quantity and value of the OWIP must be stated.

The method is known as the FIFO method because it assumes that the OWIP is completed before further production is carried out.

Example 10 OWIP – FIFO method

The data relating to a process in July was as follows:

Opening WIP: 100 units at a total cost of £310

Degree of completion:	Materials	80%
	Labour	60%
	Overhead	40%

Input during the period:

	£
Materials, 2,000 units	3,743
Labour	3,395
Overhead absorbed	2,865

Closing WIP: 200 units

Degree of completion:	Materials	75%
	Labour	50%
	Overhead	25%

Output was 1,900 finished units. Assume that there was no scrap.

You are required to prepare the process account, showing clearly the valuation of closing work in progress.

Answer and explanation

Draw up the process account for the period, entering the relevant data, as follows:

Process account

	Units	*£*		*Units*	*CPU*	*£*
OWIP	100	310	Output	1,900		
Materials	2,000	3,743	CWIP	200		
Labour		3,395				
Overhead		2,865				

Calculate the number of equivalent units produced during the period. The FIFO method requires **three** types of equivalent units:

(a) OWIP – the work done **this** period to complete the units, i.e.

Materials (remaining 20%)	100 × 20% = 20 EU
Labour (remaining 40%)	100 × 40% = 40 EU
Overhead (remaining 60%)	100 × 60% = 60 EU

(b) The **units** started and completed this period: the output was stated as 1,900 units; however, 100 units will represent the OWIP which has only been finished off this period. It is therefore the remaining 1,800 units which were both started and completed this period.

(c) CWIP – the work done **this** period, i.e.

Materials	200 × 75% = 150 EU
Labour	200 × 50% = 100 EU
Overhead	200 × 25% = 50 EU

This can be stated in summary form as:

Summary of equivalent units

	Total	*Materials*	*Labour*	*Overhead*
OWIP, to complete	100	20	40	60
Units started and completed	1,800	1,800	1,800	1,800
CWIP, started	200	150	100	50
	2,100	1,970	1,940	1,910

The total column represents the units accounted for on the credit side of the process account. The other columns represent the equivalent units of output for valuation purposes.

The costs of the work done **this** period are as follows:

Statement of costs

	Total	*Materials*	*Labour*	*Overhead*
	£	£	£	£
Input costs	10,003	3,743	3,395	2,865

It is these input costs which must be related to the work done, as shown by the equivalent units.

A format usually known as the 'evaluation statement' is very useful when dealing with work in progress. It can also manage further complications such as normal and abnormal losses and abnormal gains. It will therefore be used in these examples.

Evaluation statement

		Total	Materials	Labour	Overhead
(a)	*Costs*	£10,003	£3,743	£3,395	£2,865
(b)	*Units*				
	OWIP, to complete	100	20	40	60
	Units started and completed	1,800	1,800	1,800	1,800
	CWIP, started	200	150	100	50
		2,100	1,970	1,940	1,910
(c)	*Cost per unit*	See note 2	£1.90	£1.75	£1.50
(d)	*Evaluation*	See note 3			
		£	£	£	£
	OWIP, to complete	198	38	70	90
	Units started and completed	9,270	3,420	3,150	2,700
	CWIP, started	535	285	175	75
		10,003	3,743	3,395	2,865

Notes

1 The cost per equivalent unit must be calculated separately for each cost element

Materials $\frac{\text{£}3{,}743}{1{,}970 \text{ EU}}$ = £1.90 per EU

Labour $\frac{\text{£}3{,}395}{1{,}940 \text{ EU}}$ = £1.75 per EU

Overhead $\frac{\text{£}2{,}865}{1{,}910 \text{ EU}}$ = £1.50 per EU

2 The total cost per unit for units started and completed this period is arrived at by adding the cost elements together, i.e., £1.90 + £1.75 + £1.50 = £5.15 per finished unit.

The CPU is not arrived at by dividing the total cost of £10,003 by the total units of 2,100. This would ignore the equivalent units of production which have been so carefully calculated.

3 (i) In the evaluation statement, (d), the values in the materials, labour and overhead columns have been calculated by reference to the units in (b) and the cost per unit in (c), e.g., the materials column is calculated as:

	£
OWIP, to complete 20 × £1.90	38
Units started and completed 1,800 × £1.90	3,420
CWIP, started 150 × £1.90	285
	3,743

The process is then repeated for the labour and overhead columns.

(ii) The values in the total column have been determined by adding together across the columns the sum of the materials, labour and overhead costs calculated as in (i) above, e.g., OWIP of £198 is made up of £38 + £70 + £90.

4 These valuations can now be used to complete the process account. The CWIP can be included as stated. However, the output of 1,900 units is made up of three costs:

	£	£
(i) units started and completed this period: 1,800 × £5.15		9,270
(ii) OWIP: costs from last period	310	
(iii) costs this period (as above)	198	
		508
Cost of completed output		9,778

The completed process account will be shown as:

Process account

	Units	*£*		*Units*	*CPU*	*£*
OWIP	100	310	Output	1,900		9,778
Materials	2,000	3,743	CWIP	200		535
Labour		3,395				
Overhead		2,865				
	2,100	10,313		2,100		10,313

It is important to remember that the output in the process account is *not* valued at £5.15 per unit. This is the valuation for work started and completed this period. The 1,900 units of output also include the 100 units of OWIP which comprises both the costs from last period and the costs from this period. However, for control purposes, the value of output for the period would usually be based on £5.15 representing the cost per finished unit relating to this period.

This method is used when it is assumed that the opening work in progress will be completed during the current month.

OPENING WORK IN PROGRESS – AVERAGE METHOD

If the average method is used, the percentage degree of completion of each element of the opening work in progress will not be given, but the amount of cost incurred on each cost element to date *will* be stated.

This method is known as the average method because it averages out the costs incurred on the opening work in progress in the last period together with the costs incurred this period. In order to arrive at an average, last period's costs must therefore be included.

Example 11 OWIP – average method

The data relating to a process in August was as follows:

Opening WIP: 300 units at a total cost of £1,082

		£
Analysed as:	Material	520
	Labour	326
	Overhead	236
Input during the period:		
Material: 3,100 units		6,784
Labour		5,506
Overhead absorbed		6,084
Closing WIP: 400 units		
Degree of completion:	Materials	80%
	Labour	60%
	Overhead	40%

Output was 3,000 finished units. Assume that there was no scrap.

You are required to prepare the process account, showing clearly the valuation of closing work in progress.

Answer and explanation

Draw up the process account for the period, entering the relevant data, as follows:

Process account

	Units	£		Units	CPU	£
OWIP	300	1,082	Output	3,000		
Materials	3,100	6,784	CWIP	400		
Labour		5,506				
Overhead		6,084				

Prepare an evaluation statement. If necessary, the calculation of the equivalent units can be shown as separate workings.

Evaluation statement

	Total	Materials	Labour	Overhead
(a) *Costs* (note 1)	£	£	£	£
Input costs	18,374	6,784	5,506	6,084
OWIP	1,082	520	326	236
	19,456	7,304	5,832	6,320
(b) *Units*				
Completed units	3,000	3,000	3,000	3,000
CWIP: started (EU)	400	320	240	160
	3,400	3,320	3,240	3,160
(c) *Cost per unit* (note 2)	(note 3)	£2.2	£1.8	£2
(d) *Evaluation* (note 4)	£	£	£	£
Completed units	18,000	6,600	5,400	6,000
CWIP	1,456	704	432	320
	19,456	7,304	5,832	6,320

Notes

1 The costs which must be included are both this period's input costs and the valuation of opening work in progress, each analysed under their cost elements. When added together, they will be *averaged* out over the units produced.

2 The cost per equivalent unit must be calculated separately for each cost element.

Materials $\frac{£7,304}{3,320 \text{ EU}}$ = £2.20 per EU

Labour $\frac{£5,832}{3,240 \text{ EU}}$ = £1.80 per EU

Overhead $\frac{£6,320}{3,160 \text{ EU}}$ = £2 per EU

3 The total cost for completed units is again arrived at by adding the cost elements together, i.e. £2.20 + £1.80 + £2 = £6 per finished unit, and *not* by dividing the total costs by the total units, which would ignore the equivalent units of production.

4 (i) In the evaluation statement, (d), the values in the materials, labour and overhead columns have again been calculated by reference to the units in (b) and the cost per unit in (c), as explained in the notes to the answer for example 10.

(ii) The values in the total column have been determined by adding together across the columns the sum of the materials, labour and overhead costs calculated as in (i) above, e.g. CWIP of £1,456 is made up of £704 + £432 + £320.

The completed process account will be shown as:

Process account

	Units	*£*		*Units*	*CPU*	*£*
OWIP	300	1,082	Output	3,000	£6	18,000
Materials	3,100	6,784	CWIP	400		1,456
Labour		5,506				
Overhead		6,084				
	3,400	19,456		3,400		19,456

The valuation of the completed output and the closing work in progress was shown in the last part of the evaluation statement. Note that the completed output can be valued at £6 per unit as the costs of the OWIP have been averaged with this period's costs.

This method is used when it is assumed that the opening work in progress will be mixed in with the current month's production and cannot be separately identified.

A PREVIOUS PROCESS

In Chapter 2 it was mentioned that one of the features of process costing is that finished goods are produced from a system of separate, consecutive processes. All the examples so far have assumed that there has only been one process.

It is possible that the process which you are required to account for may not be the first process, but may be the second or third. This should cause no problems, as long as the previous process cost is regarded as a material input to the current process. Additional materials may be added in the process, but this will not usually cause any additional units to be produced. The completed units must have passed through every stage of production, from process 1 to the final process. There are a few exceptions to this. Example 15 introduces additional material into Process B. Look carefully at the information provided.

Losses and gains may occur at any stage in any process, and there may be opening and closing work in progress in any of the processes at the end of an accounting period. The principles of accounting for all these items have already been explained, so the practice of preparing the process accounts should not be too difficult.

Example 12 A previous process cost

The inputs to process 2 in September were as follows:

From process 1: 4,500 units @ £8 per unit

	£
Materials added	8,640
Labour	7,452
Overhead absorbed	6,432

Output was 3,900 units, transferred to process 3. Assume that there was no scrap.

There were 600 units of closing work in progress with the following degree of completion:

Materials	70%
Labour	40%
Overhead	20%

You are required to prepare the account for process 2 showing clearly the valuation of work in progress.

Answer and explanation

Draw up the process 2 account for the period, entering the relevant data as follows:

Process 2 account

	Units	*£*		*Units*	*CPU*	*£*
Process 1	4,500	36,000	Process 3	3,900		
Materials		8,640	CWIP	600		
Labour		7,452				
Overhead		6,432				

Prepare an evaluation statement, with an extra column for the process 1 input.

Evaluation statement

		Total	*Process 1*	*Materials*	*Labour*	*Overhead*
(a)	*Costs*	£58,524	£36,000	£8,640	£7,452	£6,432
(b)	*Units*					
	Completed units	3,900	3,900	3,900	3,900	3,900
	CWIP (note 1)	600	600	420	240	120
		4,500	4,500	4,320	4,140	4,020
(c)	*Cost per unit*	(note 2)	£8	£2	£1.80	£1.60
(d)	*Evaluation*	£	£	£	£	£
	Completed units	52,260	31,200	7,800	7,020	6,240
	CWIP	6,264	4,800	840	432	192
		58,524	36,000	8,640	7,452	6,432

Notes

1 The closing work in progress is only partially completed as far as the materials, labour and overhead in process 2 is concerned. However, it is *fully* complete as far as process 1 is concerned, as otherwise these units would not have been transferred through from process 1 to process 2.

2 The cost per unit is calculated separately for each cost element. The total cost for completed units is arrived at by adding the cost elements together, i.e., £8 + £2 + £1.80 + £1.60 = £13.40 per finished unit. Note that this is a cumulative cost and includes the cost of process 1 (£8 per unit).

The completed process account will be shown as:

Process 2 account

	Units	*£*		*Units*	*CPU*	*£*
Process 1	4,500	36,000	Process 3	3,900	£13.40	52,260
Materials		8,640	CWIP	600		6,264
Labour		7,452				
Overhead		6,432				
	4,500	58,524		4,500		58,524

EQUIVALENT UNITS, NORMAL AND ABNORMAL LOSSES

The principles outlined in Chapter 2 still apply to normal and abnormal losses, but the use of the evaluation statement where there are equivalent units of work in progress, means that the calculation of the cost per unit, based on everything that is normal, is carried out using a format different from the one described in Chapter 2.

The use of the evaluation statement means that it is easy to account for both normal and abnormal losses. These losses may be discovered:

(a) when the units are complete, i.e., at final inspection;

(b) when the units are only partially complete.

Where units are inspected during the process, defective items will be scrapped at the point of rejection.

LOSSES DISCOVERED WHEN ONLY PARTIALLY COMPLETE

As stated in Example 10, OWIP – FIFO method, the evaluation statement can manage various forms of equivalent units. The following example shows how to deal with losses or scrapped units which are discovered during the production process.

Example 13 Scrap discovered when units are partially completed

The following data relates to process 2 in November:

Transferred from process 1: 3,500 units at a cost of £15,750

Inputs during the period:

	£
Materials added	11,970
Labour	8,670
Overhead absorbed	5,520

Closing WIP: 400 units

Degree of completion:	Materials	75%
	Labour	50%
	Overhead	25%

Normal loss: A scrap allowance is made for 10% of the input from the previous process. All losses have a scrap value of £4 per unit. The units to be scrapped are discovered at the following stage of completion:

Materials	80%
Labour	60%
Overhead	40%

2,600 units were transferred to process 3.

You are required to prepare the necessary accounts for the process.

Answer and explanation

Determine whether the FIFO method or the average method of valuing opening work in progress has been used. As no percentages of completion are shown, the FIFO method cannot be used, so the average method must be employed.

Draw up the process account and enter the relevant data. Calculate the normal loss and determine whether there is an abnormal loss or an abnormal gain.

Process 2 account

	Units	*£*		*Units*	*CPU*	*£*
Process 1	3,500	15,750	Process 3	2,600		
Materials		11,970	Normal loss	350	£4	1,400
Labour		8,670	Abnormal loss	150		
Overhead		5,520	CWIP	400		

Prepare the evaluation statement, which will provide the data for completing the process account.

Evaluation statement

		Total	Process 1	Materials	Labour	Overhead
		£	£	£	£	£
(a)	*Costs*	41,910	15,750	11,970	8,670	5,520
	Normal scrap	(1,400)		(1,400)		
		40,510	15,750	10,570	8,670	5,520
(b)	*Units*					
	Completed units	2,600	2,600	2,600	2,600	2,600
	CWIP	400	400	300	200	100
	Normal loss	350	–	–	–	–
	Abnormal loss	150	150	120	90	60
		3,500	3,150	3,020	2,890	2,760
(c)	*Cost per unit*	£13.50	£5	£3.50	£3	£2
(d)	*Evaluation*	£	£	£	£	£
	Completed units	35,100	13,000	9,100	7,800	5,200
	CWIP	3,850	2,000	1,050	600	200
	Normal loss	–	–	–	–	–
	Abnormal loss	1,560	750	420	270	120
		40,510	15,750	10,570	8,670	5,520

Notes

1 In Chapter 2 the normal scrap proceeds were used to reduce the cost of production. The same principle is followed here, but more specifically the normal scrap proceeds are used to reduce the *material* cost of production, for evaluation purposes only.

2 The 'units' part, (b), is prepared in the usual way, showing completed units and closing work in progress. The cost per unit calculation is based on everything that is normal. For this reason the normally lost units are excluded from the evaluation. Remember that the only value a normal loss ever has is its scrap value.

The abnormal loss is included in the evaluation in (b) and (d) as abnormal losses (and gains) should be stated at the cost per unit. If these units are to share in the costs, then they must be included in (b), 'units', remembering to include the appropriate number of equivalent units.

Next, complete the process account.

Process account

	Units	*£*		*Units*	*CPU*	*£*
Process 1	3,500	15,750	Process 3	2,600	£13.50	35,100
Materials		11,970	Normal loss	350	£ 4	1,400
Labour		8,670	Abnormal loss	150		1,560
Overhead		5,520	CWIP	400		3,850
	3,500	41,910		3,500		41,910

Note that the abnormal loss is not allocated a cost per unit in the process account. Why not? The reason is that the 150 units were scrapped when only partially complete, and at various stages of completion for the different cost elements. The valuation is similar to that of CWIP, which is also not allocated a cost per unit, as it is only partially completed.

Finally, complete the normal and abnormal loss accounts, using double entry principles.

Normal loss account

	Units	*CPU*	*£*		*Units*	*CPU*	*£*
Process account	350	£4	1,400	Bank	350	£4	1,400

Abnormal loss account

	Units	CPU	£		Units	CPU	£
Process account	150		1,560	Bank	150	£4	600
				Profit & loss			960
	150		1,560		150		1,560

Note that the charge to the profit and loss account is made up as:

	£
Cost of abnormal loss 150 units	1,560
Less: scrap value of abnormal loss 150 × £4	600
Net cost of abnormal loss	960

Chapter 4

Process Costing Examples

Example 14

A firm operates a process, the details of which for the period were as follows:

- There was no opening work-in-progress.
- During the period 8,250 units were received from the previous process at a value of £453,750, labour and overheads were £350,060 and material introduced was £24,750.
- At the end of the period the closing work in progress was 1,600 units, which were 100% complete in respect of materials, and 60% complete in respect of labour and overheads.
- The balance of units were transferred to finished goods.

Requirements

(a)	Calculate the number of equivalent units produced.	3 marks
(b)	Calculate the cost per equivalent unit.	2 marks
(c)	Prepare the process account.	7 marks
		Total marks = 12

Answer and explanation

Although the process account requirement is (c), it would be helpful to prepare an outline process account at this stage.

Process account

	Units	*£*		*Units*	*CPU*	*£*
Previous process	8,250	453,750	CWIP	1,600		
Labour and overhead		350,060	Finished goods	6,650		
Additional material		24,750				
	8,250	£828,560		8,250		

This shows that the number of finished units was 6,650, with 1,600 units of closing work in progress.

(a) and (b) can be calculated by means of the evaluation statement, which will also provide all the necessary information for the process account.

Evaluation statement

		Total	*Previous process*	*Additional material*	*Labour and overhead*
(a)	*Costs*	£828,560	£453,750	£24,750	£350,060
(b)	*Units*				
	Completed units	6,650	6,650	6,650	6,650
	CWIP	1,600	1,600	1,600	960
		8,250	8,250	8,250	7,610
(c)	*Cost per unit*	£104	£55	£3	£46
(d)	*Evaluation*	£	£	£	£
	Completed units	691,600	365,750	19,950	305,900
	CWIP	136,960	88,000	4,800	44,160
		828,560	453,750	24,750	350,060

Notes

1 The fact that labour and overhead are shown as a total cost simply means that the evaluation statement is adapted to show a column with this heading. This may be done if the percentage completion of the cost elements is the same. The evaluation statement will always have a heading for each category of cost.

2 The total cost per unit is determined in the normal way, by adding together the individual elements of cost: £55 + £3 + £46 = £104.

3 In examinations the individual elements of cost, which combine to give the total cost per unit, are usually 'round numbers'. If this is not the case, it is worth checking the data and the calculations.

To answer the question precisely:

(a) **Equivalent units produced**

	Completed	CWIP	Total
Previous process	6,650	1,600	8,250
Materials	6,650	1,600	8,250
Labour and overhead	6,650	960	7,610

(b) **Cost per equivalent unit**

	Period cost	*Equivalent units*	*Cost per unit*
	£		£
Previous process	453,750	8,250	55
Materials	24,750	8,250	3
Labour and overhead	350,060	7,610	46
			104

Process account

	Units	*£*		*Units*	*CPU*	*£*
Previous process	8,250	453,750	CWIP	1,600		136,960
Labour and overhead		350,060	Finished goods	6,650	£104	691,600
Additional material		24,750				
	8,250	828,560		8,250		828,560

Note the closing work in progress in the process account can be shown at a cost of £85.60 per unit.

Example 15

A chemical compund is made by raw material being processed through two processes. The output of Process A is passed to Process B where further material is added to the mix. The details of the process costs for the financial period number 10 were as shown below:

Process A

Direct material	2,000 kilograms at £5 per kg
Direct labour	£7,200
Process plant time	140 hours at £60 per hour

Process B

Direct material	1,400 kilograms at £12 per kg
Direct labour	£4,200
Process plant time	80 hours at £72.50 per hour

The departmental overhead for Period 10 was £6,840 and is absorbed into the costs of each process on direct labour cost.

	Process A	*Process B*
Expected output was	80% of input	90% of input
Actual output was	1,400 kgs	2,620 kgs

Assume no finished stock at the beginning of the period and no work in progress at either the beginning or the end of the period.

Normal loss is contaminated material which is sold as scrap for £0.50 per kg from Process A and £1.825 per kg from Process B, for both of which immediate payment is received.

You are required to prepare the accounts for Period 10, for

(i) Process A,
(ii) Process B,
(iii) Normal loss/gain,
(iv) Abnormal loss/gain,
(v) Finished goods,
(vi) Profit and loss (extract). *5 marks*

Answer and explanation

It will be helpful to prepare the accounts for Process A and Process B at this stage, although they will be incomplete.

Process A account

	kgs	*£*		*kgs*	*CPU*	*£*
Direct material	2,000	10,000	Process B	1,400		
Direct labour		7,200	Normal loss	400	£0.50	200
Process plant time		8,400	Abnormal loss	200		
Overhead absorbed		4,320				
	2,000			2,000		

Process B account

	kgs	*CPU*	*£*		*kgs*	*CPU*	*£*
Process A	1,400			Finished goods	2,620		
Direct material	1,400		16,800	Normal loss	280	£1.825	511
Direct labour			4,200	Process plant time			5,800
Overhead absorbed			2,520				
Abnormal gain	100						
	2,900				2,900		

Notes

1 The overhead of £6,840 is absorbed in proportion to the total direct labour cost £7,200 + £4,200 = £11,400

$$\frac{\text{Overhead}}{\text{Direct labour}} = \frac{£6{,}840}{£11{,}400}$$ which gives a rate of 60%

of the direct labour cost of each process

Overhead absorbed:
Process A 60% of £7,200 = £4,320
Process B 60% of £4,200 = £2,520

2 The normal loss is calculated as:
Process A 20% of 2,000 kg = 400 kg
Process B 10% of 2,800 kg = 280 kg

It is important to remember that the input to Process B comprises 1,400 kg transferred from Process A and a further 1,400 kg of additional material.

3 In each process the normal loss has a scrap value which must be accounted for in the process accounts.

4 The abnormal loss in Process A occurs because the actual output (1,400 kgs) is *less* than the expected output (1,600 kg). The abnormal gain in Process B occurs because the actual output (2,620 kg) is *greater* than the expected output (2,520 kg). It is not unusual, in a question with two process accounts, to find that one process involves an abnormal loss and the other process involves an abnormal gain.

5 The cost of the transfer of 1,400 kg from Process A into Process B cannot be determined until the cost per unit in Process A has been calculated.

6 It is not necessary to prepare an evaluation statement for this example, as there are no partially completed units to account for.

7 All that is needed now is to calculate the cost per unit for each process, based on *everything that is normal* – normal costs, normal scrap proceeds, normal output.

Process A $$\frac{\text{Normal costs less normal scrap proceeds}}{\text{Normal output}}$$

$$= \frac{£10{,}000 + £7{,}200 + £8{,}400 + £4{,}320 - £200}{1{,}600\text{ kg}} = \frac{£29{,}720}{1{,}600\text{ kg}}$$

$$= £18{,}575 \text{ per unit}$$

The Process A account can now be completed:

(i) *Process A account*

	kg	£		kg	CPU	£
Direct material	2,000	10,000	Process B	1,400	£18.575	26,005
Direct labour		7,200	Normal loss	400	£0.50	200
Process plant time		8,400	Abnormal loss	200	£18.575	3,715
Overhead absorbed		4,320				
	2,000	29,920		2,000		29,920

The cost per unit is used for both the output from Process A and for the valuation of the abnormal loss in the process account. It is necessary to calculate the cost of the transfer from Process A to Process B before completing the Process B account.

Process B account

	kg	CPU	£		kg	CPU	£
Process A	1,400		26,005	Finished goods	2,620		
Direct materials	1,400		16,800	Normal loss	280	£1.825	511
Direct labour			4,200				
Process plant time			5,800				
Overhead absorbed			2,520				
Abnormal gain	100						
	2,900				2,900		

Cost per unit $\dfrac{\text{Normal costs less normal scrap proceeds}}{\text{Normal output}}$

$$= \frac{£26{,}005 + £16{,}800 + £4{,}200 + £5{,}800 + £2{,}520 - £511}{2{,}520 \text{ kg}} = \frac{£54{,}814}{2{,}520 \text{ kg}}$$

$= £21.75$ per unit

The Process B account can now be completed:

(ii) *Process B account*

	kg	CPU	£		kg	CPU	£
Process A	1,400		26,005	Finished goods	2,620	£21.75	56,989
Direct materials	1,400		16,800	Normal loss	280	£1.825	511
Direct labour			4,200				
Process plant time			5,800				
Overhead absorbed			2,520				
Abnormal gain	100	£21.75	2,175				
	2,900		57,500		2,900		57,500

This is an example of an examination question which does *not* result in a 'round number' cost per unit. As the cost per unit of £21.75 has been rounded down, the finished goods valuation must be rounded up from 2,620 x £21.75 = £56,985 to £56,989 for the process account to balance.

(iii) *Normal loss account*

	kg	*CPU*	*£*		*kg*	*CPU*	*£*
Process A account	400	£0.50	200	Bank (A)	600	£0.50	300.0
Process B account	280	£1.825	511	Bank (B)	180	£1.825	328.5
Abnormal loss (A)	200	£0.50	100	Abnormal gain (B)	100	£1.825	182.5
	880		811		880		811.0

(iv) *Abormal loss/gain account*

	kg	*CPU*	*£*		*kg*	*CPU*	*£*
Process A account	200	£18.575	3,715	Process B account	100	£21.75	2,175
Normal loss (B)	100	£1.825	182.5	Normal loss (A)	200	£0.50	100
				Profit and loss			1,622.5
	300		3,897. 5		300		3,897.5

The completion of the normal loss account and the abnormal loss/gain account needs careful consideration. The abnormal loss/gain account is simply a combination of the abnormal loss account and the abnormal gains account.

When completing the normal loss account, work through these stages:

1 Complete the double entry from the process accounts;
2 Credit the **actual** scrap sold;
3 Transfer any balance from each process to the abnormal loss/gain account as it represents additional scrap because of an abnormal loss or a shortage of scrap because of an abnormal gain;
4 Check that the normal loss account now balances for both units at £.

When completing the abnormal loss/gain account, work through these stages:

1 Complete the double entry from the process accounts;
2 Complete the double entry from the normal loss accounts;
3 The balance will represent the transfer to the profit and loss account.

The transfer to the profit of loss account of £1,622.50 can be checked thus:

			£	£
Process A	– Abnormal loss	200 kg × £18.575	3,715	
	– Scrap proceeds	200 kg × £0.50	100	
	Net loss			3,615
Process B	– Abnormal gain	100 × £21.75	2,175	
	– Loss of scrap proceeds	100 × £1.825	182.5	
	Net gain			(1,992.5)
Overall loss				1,622.50

(v) *Finished goods account*

	kg	*CPU*	*£*
Process B account	2,620	£21.75	56,989

(vi) *Profit and loss account*

	£
Abnormal loss/gain account	1,622.5

These last two accounts involve completing the double entry from Process B account and the abnormal loss/gain account.

Example 16

ABC Limited operates an integrated accounting system. It is a chemical processing company, which converts three raw materials – W, X and Y – into a final product Z through two consecutive processes. Product Z is used as a fertiliser in the farming industry.

On 30 September an extract of the trial balance taken from its ledgers was as follows:

	£	£
Raw material control account	15,400	
Work in progress control account	21,520	
Production overhead control account		2,360
Abnormal loss account	1,685	
Abnormal gain account		930
Finished goods control account	27,130	

The following notes are also relevant:

1 ABC Limited prepares its financial accounts to 31 October each year.

2 The raw material control account balance comprises:

Direct materials:		£
Material X	4,200 kg @ £2 per kg	8,400
Material Y	1,050 kg @ £4 per kg	4,200
Indirect materials		2,800
		15,400

3 The work in progress control account balance comprises:

Process 2	8,400 kg	Process 1	8,720
		Materials	2,000
		Labour	3,600
		Overhead	7,200
			21,520

During October, the following transactions occurred:

(i) Indirect materials purchased on credit amounted to £1,300.

(ii) Direct materials were purchased on credit as follows:

Material W	10,500 kg costing	£4,960
Material X	10,000 kg costing	£21,000
Material Y	5,000 kg costing	£19,000

(iii) Direct wages were incurred as follows:

Process 1	£17,160
Process 2	£8,600

(iv) Indirect wages were incurred amounting to £2,980.

(v) Production overhead costs incurred (excluding materials and labour costs) amounted to £31,765.

(vi) Indirect materials consumed in the month amounted to £1,450.

(vii) Direct materials were issued to production as follows:

Process 1	10,500 kg of W costing	£4,960
	7,200 kg of X costing	£14,700
Process 2	4,050 kg of Y costing	£15,600

There was no opening or closing stock of material W.

(viii) The cost of finished goods sold during the month amounted to £125,740.

The completed output from the two processes for October amounted to:

Process 1	13,100 kg
Process 2	20,545 kg

Closing work-in-progress, which is 100% complete as to materials but only 50% completed as to conversion cost, amounted to:

Process 1	2,000 kg
Process 2	1,500 kg

Normal losses, caused by evaporation and occurring at the end of processing, are expected in each of the processes as follows:

Process 1	15% throughput
Process 2	10% of throughput

Note: Throughput equals opening work in progress plus materials introduced less closing work in progress.

Production overhead is absorbed using the following absorption rates:

Process 1	150% of direct labour cost
Process 2	200% of direct labour cost

Requirements:

(a) Prepare the accounts for EACH of the TWO processes for the month of October. *16 marks*

(b) Prepare the SIX ledger accounts for which opening balances have been given, commencing with those balances, entering the transactions for the month of October and making entries in those accounts for 31 October as appropriate. *9 marks*

(c) State the differences between using an integrated accounting system compared to an interlocking system, and explain the advantages and disadvantages caused by those differences. *5 marks*

Total marks = 30

Answer and explanation

(a) **Process Accounts**

It is helpful to prepare an outline account for each process at this stage. These can then be completed as the necessary information is calculated.

Process 1 account

	kg	*£*		*kg*	*CPU*	*£*
Raw mat'ls control						
– Material W	10,500	4,960	Process 2	13,100		
– Material X	7,200	14,700	CWIP	2,000		
Wages control		17,160	Normal loss	2,355	–	–
Prod'n o/h control		25,740	Abnormal loss	245		
	17,700			17,700		

Notes

1 As the question also involves the use of an integrated accounting system, the correct double entry terms have been used.

2 Every process account will normally comprise materials, labour and overhead costs. Check through the data carefully and make sure that these have been included.

3 Production overhead is absorbed at 150% of direct labour cost.

4 The normal loss is caculated as 15% of the throughput, i.e. opening work in progress plus materials introduced less closing work in progress. In this example:

$$(0 + 10.500 \text{ kg} + 7{,}200 \text{ kg} - 2{,}000 \text{ kg}) \times 15\% = 2{,}355 \text{ kg}$$

5 As the normal loss is caused by evaporation, there is no scrap value.

6 The closing work in progress involves partially completed units, therefore an evaluation statement is used.

Evaluation statement

		Total	*Raw materials*	*Wages*	*Production overhead*
		£	£	£	£
(a)	*Costs*	62,560	19,660	17,160	25,740
(b)	*Units*				
	Completed units	13,100	13,100	13,100	13,100
	CWIP	2,000	2,000	1,000	1,000
	Abnormal loss	245	245	245	245
		15,345	15,345	14,345	14,345
(c)	*Cost per unit*	£4.2716	£1.2812	£1.196	£1.7944
(d)	*Evaluation*	£	£	£	£
	Completed units	55,961	16,784	15,671	23,506
	CWIP	5,552	2,562	1,196	1,794
	Abnormal loss	1,047	314	293	440
		£62,560	£19,660	£17,160	£25,740

This information can now be used to complete the account for Process 1.

Process 1 account

	kg	£		kg	CPU(£)	£
Raw mat'ls control			Process 2	13,100	4.2716	55,961
– Material W	10,500	4,960	CWIP	2,000		5,552
– Material X	7,200	14,700	Normal loss	2,355	–	–
Wages control		17,160	Abnormal loss	245		1,047
Prod'n o/h control		25,740				
	17,700	62,560		17,700		62,560

Following the same procedures for Process 2

Process 2 account

	kg	£		kg	CPU	£
OWIP	8,400	21,520	Finished goods	20,545		
Process 1	13,100	55,961	Normal loss	2,405	–	–
Raw mat'ls control			CWIP	1,500		
– Material Y	4,050	15,600	Abnormal loss	1,100		
Wages control		8,600				
Prod'n o/h control		17,200				
	25,550			25,550		

Notes

1 Production overhead is absorbed at 200% of direct labour cost.

2 The normal loss is calculated as 10% of the throughput, i.e. opening work in progress plus materials introduced less closing work in progress. In this example:

$$(8{,}400 \text{ kg} + 13{,}100 \text{ kg} + 4{,}050 \text{ kg} - 1{,}500 \text{ kg}) \times 10\% = 2{,}405 \text{ kg}$$

3 As the normal loss is caused by evaporation, there is no scrap value.

4 The closing work in progress involves partially completed units, therefore an evaluation statement is used.

5 The opening work in progress as shown does not include the percentage degree of completion, so the **average** method must be used.

Evaluation statement

	Total	Process 1	Raw materials	Wages	Production overhead
	£	£	£	£	£
(a) *Costs*					
OWIP	21,520	8,720	2,000	3,600	7,200
Input costs	97,361	55,961	15,600	8,600	17,200
	118,881	64,681	17,600	12,200	24,400
(b) *Units*					
Output	20,545	20,545	20,545	20,545	20,545
CWIP	1,500	1,500	1,500	750	750
Abnormal loss	1,100	1,100	1,100	1,100	1,100
	23,145	23,145	23,145	22,395	22,395
(c) *Cost per unit*	5.1893	2.7946	0.7604	0.5448	1.0895
(d) *Evaluation*					
Output	106,614	57,415	15,623	11,192	22,384
CWIP	6,559	4,192	1,141	409	817
Abnormal loss	5,708	3,074	836	599	1,199
	118,881	64,681	17,600	12,200	24,400

Note that the cost per unit figures are rounded, and some rounding must also be used in the evaluation so that the process account will balance.

This information can now be used to complete the process account.

Process 2 account

	kg	£		kg	CPU (£)	£
OWIP	8,400	21,520	Finished goods	20,545	5.189	106,614
Process 1	13,100	55,961	Normal loss	2,405	–	–
Raw mat'ls control			CWIP	1,500		6,559
- Material Y	4,050	15,600	Abnormal loss	1,100	5.189	5,708
Wages control		8,600				
Prod'n o/h control		17,200				
	25,550	118,881		25,550		118,881

(b) Ledger Accounts

This section is useful practice in accounting for costs.

Raw material control account

	£		£
Balance b/f	15,400	Prod'n overhead control **(vi)**	1,450
Creditors control**(i) (ii)**	46,260	Work in progress control **(vii)**	35,260
		Balance c/f	24,950
	61,660		61,660

Work in progress control account

Balance b/f	21,520	Finished goods control **(note 3)**	106,614
Raw material control **(vii)**	35,260	Abnormal loss **(note 4)**	6,755
Wages control **(iii)**	25,760	Balance c/f	12,111
Production o/h control **(note 2)**	42,940		
	125,480		125,480

Production overhead control account

Raw material control **(vi)**	1,450	Balance b/f	2,360
Wages control **(iv)**	2,980	WIP control **(note 2)**	42,940
Cost ledger control **(v)**	31,765		
Profit and loss	9,105		
	45,300		45,300

Abnormal loss account

Balance b/f	1,685	Profit and loss	8,440
Work in progress control **(note 4)**	6,755		
	8,440		8,440

Abnormal gain account

Profit and loss	930	Balance b/f	930

Finished goods control account

Balance b/f	27,130	Cost of sales **(viii)**	125,740
Work in progress control **(note 3)**	106,614	Balance c/f	8,004
	133,744		133,744

Notes

1 The roman numbers relate to the transactions detailed in the example.

2 Production overhead is debited to the work in progress account and credited to the production overhead control account as:

Process 1	25,740
Process 2	17,200
	42,940

3 The finished goods are as shown in the account for Process 2.

4 The abnormal loss comprises:

Process 1	1,047
Process 2	5,708
	6,755

(c) Integrated and interlocking accounting systems

In an integrated accounting system, the cost accounting records and the financial accounting records are contained within a single set of accounts.

In an interlocking accounting system, two separate sets of accounting records are required, one for producing costing information and the other for producing financial accounting information.

The advantages of the integrated system are that data is entered only once, rather than twice and that it is not necessary to prepare periodic reconciliations of the two sets of records. The main disadvantage of the integrated system is that financial accounting standards and regulations determine the information produced by the accounting system and this may not be appropriate data on which managers should base their decisions.

Chapter 5

Joint and By-product Costing

INTRODUCTION

Joint costs arise in several situations, for example, in absorbing overhead costs to products. However, this chapter concentrates on one particular aspect of joint costs, that of a common production process which results in more than one end product. This situation will occur where the production of one product automatically results in the production of other products.

Joint products are defined as 'two or more products separated in processing, each having a sufficiently high saleable value to merit recognition as a main product' (CIMA *Terminology*, p. 43).

A **by-product** is defined as 'output of some value produced incidentally in manufacturing something else (main product)'. (CIMA *Terminology*, p. 31).

This is shown in Figure 5.1.

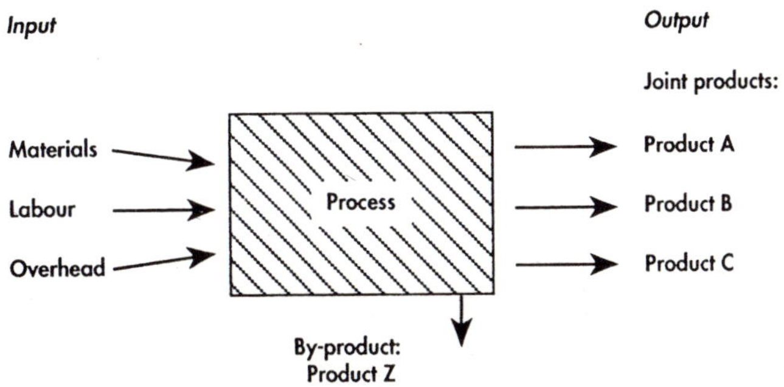

Figure 5.1 Joint products and by-products

It is important to realise that it is the **relative sales value** of the output which will determine whether any product is to be regarded as a joint product or as a by-product, *not* the manufacturing process. For example, some firms are extracting both oil and gas from the North Sea. Provided that the sales values of the two products are relatively similar, these will be considered as joint products. In other countries, the same process may result in the same products, but whereas the oil is sold, the gas may be burnt as it is extracted, because the country does not have the technology to utilise the gas. In this case, the gas is not even a by-product, as it has no realisable value, but is waste.

Although the joint costs are considered to be common to the joint products, further work may be carried out on one or more of the products in order to make them ready for sale. The point at which the specific products can be identified is known as the **split off point** and the further work carried out will be identified in terms of **additional processing costs.**

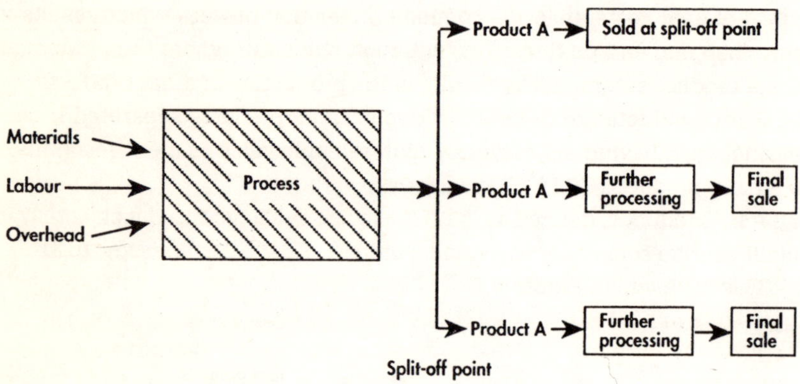

Figure 5.2 Split off point

Products A, B and C emerge from the process. The sales value of each determines that they are to be regarded as joint products. Product A is sold at its **split-off point**, but Products B and C undergo further processing before being sold.

Joint product costing examples normally relate to either or both of two distinct areas:

(a) stock valuation for profit determination: this requires the costs of the process to be shared between the joint products;

(b) determining whether it is profitable to process further any of the products in order to increase the sales value: this requires the use of the incremental approach to decision-making.

THE APPORTIONMENT OF JOINT COSTS FOR STOCK VALUATION PURPOSES

It is important to understand that it is only necessary to apportion the costs of the process to the end products in order to value stock, which in turn, is required to determine the profit for the period.

There are two main methods of doing this:

(a) the physical measure basis;

(b) the sales value basis.

There is also a third method which should be used when one or more of the products has to undergo further processing before being sold. This has a variety of names, for example:

(c) the net realisable sales value method or the notional sales value method.

THE PHYSICAL MEASURES BASIS

This is usually the easiest method to use whereby the process costs are apportioned according to the physical measure of output.

Example 17

A chemical process produces two products, Wye and Zed. The joint costs of the process are £2,000. Output is 400kg of Wye, which is sold for £6 per kg and 100kg of Zed which is sold for £8 per kg. There is no scrap.

(a) You are required to apportion the joint costs using the physical measures basis.

(b) Assuming that 100kg of Wye and 10kg of Zed remain unsold at the end of the accounting period, prepare a statement showing the profit from Wye and from Zed and the total profit for the period.

Answer and explanation

It is sometimes helpful to show the process by means of a diagram, as in Figure 5.3.

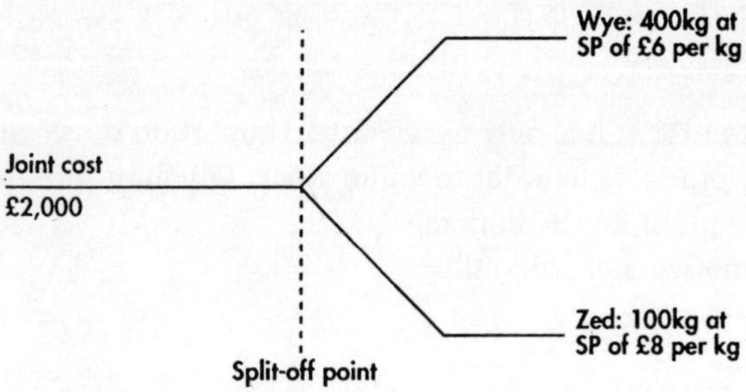

Figure 5.3

(a) **Apportionment of joint costs**:

Product	*Physical measure*	*Weighting*	*Joint costs apportioned*	*Cost per unit*
	kg		£	£
Wye	400	400/500 × £2,000	1,600	4
Zed	100	100/500 × £2,000	400	4
	500		2,000	

(b) **Profit statement**:

	Wye		*Zed*		*Total*	
	£	£	£	£	£	£
Sales revenue		1,800		720		2,520
Cost of production	1,600		400		2,000	
Less: Closing stock	400		40		440	
Cost of sales		1,200		360		1,560
Gross profit		600		360		960
Gross profit percentage		33⅓%		50%		38%

Notes

1. The split-off point is where separate products become physically identifiable.
2. The cost per unit of £4 per kg, which is used for stock valuation purposes, is calculated by dividing the joint costs apportioned to the product by the kilograms of output.
3. When using the physical measures basis for apportioning joint costs, the cost per unit will be the same for both products, provided there are no additional processing costs.
4. The total column in the profit statement is determined by adding together the values for the individual products.

The sales value method

This method is called the sales value method because it relates to the sales value of *production*. It is important to understand that this is not the same as sales revenue, which is the value of sales turnover. The distinction is important where production and sales are not equal, i.e., where there is closing stock.

Example 18

Using the data provided in Example 17.

(a) You are required to apportion the joint costs using the sales value basis.

(b) Assuming that 100kg of Wye and 10kg of Zed remain unsold at the end of the accounting period, prepare a statement showing the profit from Wye and from Zed and the total profit for the period.

Answer and explanation

It is again helpful to show the process by means of a diagram, but this time with the addition of sales values of production (Figure 5.4).

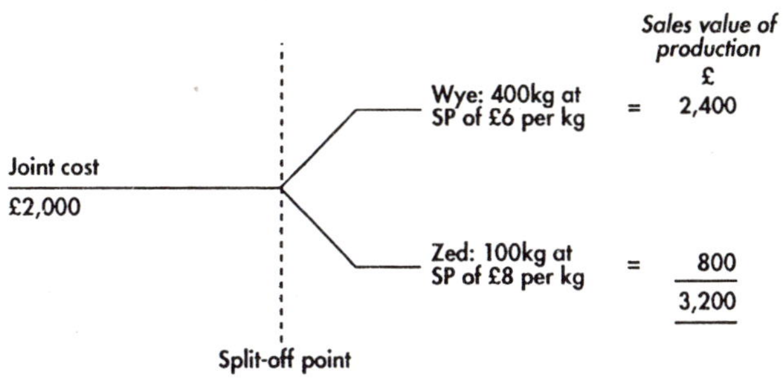

Figure 5.4

(a) **Apportionment of joint costs:**

Product	*Sales value of production*	*Weighting*	*Joint costs apportioned*	*Cost per unit*
	£		£	£
Wye	2,400	2,400/3,200 × £2,000	1,500	3.75
Zed	800	800/3,200 × £2,000	500	5.00
	3;200		2,000	

(b) **Profit statement:**

	Wye		*Zed*		*Total*	
	£	£	£	£	£	£
Sales revenue		1,800		720		2,520
Cost of production	1,500		500		2,000	
Less: Closing stock	375		50		425	
Cost of sales		1,125		450		1,575
Gross profit		675		270		945
Gross profit percentage		37.5		37.5		37.5

Notes

1 The cost of production is based on the sales value method of apportioning joint costs, as in (a).

2 The cost per unit for each product, which is used for stock valuation puposes, is calculated by dividing the joint costs apportioned to the product by the output (in units or kilograms). Errors are common with this calculation. With the sales value method, the joint costs are provided in the apportionment of joint costs statement, but the output is *not*.

3 When using the sales value basis for apportioning joint costs, the gross profit percentages for each product and in total, will be the same provided there are no additional processing costs.

There are disadvantages with both the physical measures and the sales value methods of apportioning joint costs to products.

With the physical measures basis, it is possible for the product with the greatest costs to have the lowest revenue and for it to seem as if that product is making a loss. This would occur where its cost per unit is higher than its sales value per unit.

It can be argued that the sales value method is simply a method of apportioning profits, as the cost is determined by the sales value, but it does overcome the major drawback of the physical measures basis.

The notional or net realisable sales value method

In a slightly more complicated process, one or more of the joint products may have to undergo further processing before it can be sold, as it cannot be sold immediately after the split-off point. In this case, the notional or net realisable sales value method must be used.

Example 19

A chemical company produces two products, known as C15 and M16, from a common process. The total costs of the common process in June amount to £8,500. Output was 100kg of C15 and 150kg of M16. Sales during June were 80kg of C15 for £7,200 and 120kg of M16 for £9,600. There was no opening stock and no scrap. Both products have to undergo further processing before they can be sold. The separable costs of production relating to the total output from the process are as follows:

C15	£3,200
M16	£5,100

(a) You are required to apportion the joint costs using the notional or net realisable sales value basis.

(b) Prepare a profit statement showing the profit for the period from each product and in total.

Answer and explanation

The notional or net realisable sales value basis requires the joint cost to be apportioned to the products according to a notional sales value at the split-off point. The problem is that there is no actual sales value at the split-off point, as both products have to undergo further processing before they can be sold. This method arrives at a notional sales value at the split-off point by deducting the additional processing costs from the final sales value.

Figure 5.5 may help to clarify the idea.

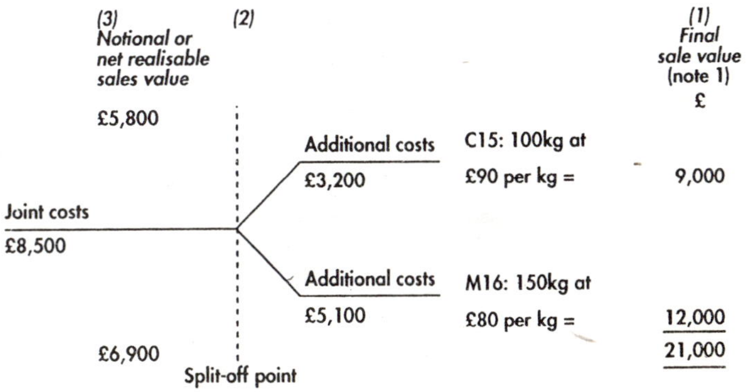

Figure 5.5

(a) **Apportionment of joint costs**:

Product	*Final sales value*	*Additional processing costs*	*Notional sales value*	*Weighting*	*Joint costs assigned*	*Cost per unit*
	£	£	£		£	£
C15	9,000	3,200	5,800	58/127 × £8,500	3,882	38.82 + 32.00
M16	12,000	5,100	6,900	69/127 × £8,500	4,618	30.79 + 34.00
	21,000	8,300	12,700		8,500	

Notes

1 The information in the question does not give the final sales value of production. This must be calculated by determining the selling price per kg and multiplying by the amount of production in the period.
2 The notional or net relative sales value is calculated by deducting the additional processing costs from the final sales value of each product.
3 The weighting of the joint costs is based on the notional or net relative sales value of production.
4 The cost per unit, for stock valuation purposes, is made up of two parts:
   (i) the share of the joint costs; and
   (ii) the additional processing costs per unit.

(b) **Profit statement**:

	C15		*M16*		*Total*	
	£	£	£	£	£	£
Sales revenue		7,200		9,600		16,800
Production costs						
Joint costs	3,882		4,618		8,500	
Separable costs	3,200		5,100		8,300	
	7,082		9,718		16,800	
Less: closing stock	1,416		1,944		3,360	
Cost of sales		5,666		7,774		13,440
Gross profit		1,534		1,826		3,360
Gross profit percentage		21.3%		19.0%		20.0%

Notes

1 Do not forget that there are now two types of production costs, i.e., the joint costs and the separable costs.

2 The closing stock valuation is calculated as:
C15 20kg × (£38.82 + £32) = £1,416
M16 30 kg × (£30.79 + £34) = £1,944
3 The gross profit percentage will not be the same for each product and in total because of the incidence of the additional processing costs.
4 Remember that the notional or net relative sales value method must be used where the products have to undergo further processing before being sold.
5 If there is a choice, and the products can be sold *either* at the split-off point *or* after further processing, the most suitable methods are the physical measures or sales value methods, as described earlier. There is no need to use the notional sales value method when all the products can be sold at the split-off point.

FURTHER PROCESSING DECISIONS

The second distinct area of problems on joint product costs often relates to whether it is profitable to process further any of the products in order to increase their sales value.

This implies that there is an option, either to sell at the split-off point or to process further. In many ways, this is often the quickest and easiest part of the example and is solved by using the incremental approach to decisions, comparing additional costs incurred with additional revenue earned. There is no need to start by apportioning joint product costs to the products, indeed the methods of appointing joint costs would not usually be relevant for this purpose.

Example 20
Walters Ltd operates a manufacturing process which jointly produces three products A, B and C. The manufacturing costs are £5,000 per week, and this produces:

1,000kg of X, which sells for £1 per kg
1,500kg of Y, which sells for £2 per kg
2,000kg of Z, which sells for £2.50 per kg

The company is considering adopting a further process which would refine products X and Y into X^1 and Y^1 and would increase their selling prices to £1.75 and £3 per kg respectively. The costs of the refining process are £800 for X and £1,250 for Y each week.

You are required to advise the firm whether the refining process will be profitable for each product.

Answer and explanation

The problem is solved by comparing the additional weekly revenue with the additional weekly costs for each product.

	Product X	Product Y
Additional revenue	(£1.75 – £1) 1,000kg	(£3 – £2) 1,500kg
	£750	£1,500
Additional costs	£800	£1,250
Additional profit (loss)	(£50)	£250

It would therefore be most profitable for the firm to process product Y further and to sell product X at the split-off point. This would increase total profits by £250 per week.

Notes

1 The current weekly profit has not been calculated, as it was not required.

2 There is no need to apportion the joint process costs to the individual products, unless specifically requested to do so.

BY-PRODUCT COSTING

The major difference between a joint product and a by-product is the relative sales value of the output. With joint products, the sales values are fairly similar, whereas with a by-product its net realisable value is small compared with that of the other products.

There is no golden rule for this test. It is a matter of judgement and experience. Consider the following net realisable values of products:

	Product A	*Product B*	*Product C*
Scenario 1	£100,000	£80,000	£50,000
Scenario 2	£100,000	£50,000	£20,000
Scenario 3	£100,000	£50,000	£10,000
Scenario 4	£100,000	£50,000	£ 1,000
Scenario 5	£100,000	£50,000	£ 100

At what point does product C become a by-product rather than a joint product? It is certainly a by-product in scenario 5 and certainly a joint product in scenarios 1 and 2. The writer's view is that it is probably a joint product in scenario 3 and probably a by-product in scenario 4. However, this is purely a matter of judgement.

ACCOUNTING FOR BY-PRODUCTS

It is important to distinguish joint products from by-products because of the different accounting treatment which they require. Whereas the joint products *do* share in the common process costs, by-products do not. Mainly because of the small net realisable value, it is not considered worthwhile to apportion a share of the joint costs to the by-products. The only costs which are ever assigned to by-products are their own further processing or packaging costs.

There are three quite common methods of accounting for by-products:

(a) Net realisable value of the by-product is shown as a deduction from the cost of production of the major products.

(b) Net realisable value of the by-product is shown as a deduction from the cost of sales of the major products.

(c) Net realisable value of the by-product is shown as 'other income' and is credited to the profit and loss account.

Example 21

Process H23 produces a main product M and a by-product B. By-product B is processed further before it can be sold. During August, the following data relates to the process:

Total costs of the process: £12,150

	Product M	Product B
Production (units)	12,000	1,000
Sales (units)	10,000	900
Selling price per unit	£ 1.50	£0.20
Further processing costs per unit		£0.05

You are required to prepare statements showing the profit for the period, assuming that the net realisable value of the by-product is shown as:

(a) a deduction from the cost of production;

(b) a deduction from the cost of sales.

Answer and explanation

First determine the net realisable value of the by-product. Note that it is not necessary to account for stocks of the by-product, and the net realisable value relates to the **sales value of production** net of any additional processing, packaging or selling costs.

		£
Sales value of product B	1,000 × £0.20	200
Further processing costs	1,000 × £0.05	50
Net realisable value		150

(a) NRV shown as a deduction from the cost of production:
This is the same treatment that is used for scrap in process costing (see Chapter 2, Process accounts with normal losses).

	Units	£
Sales revenue of product M	10,000	15,000
Cost of production:		
Production costs	12,000	12,150
Less: NRV of by-product B		150
		12,000
Less: Closing stock of product M	2,000	2,000
Cost of sales	10,000	10,000
Gross profit		5,000

(b) NRV shown as a deduction from the cost of sales

	Units	£
Sales revenue of product M	10,000	15,000
Production costs	12,000	12,150
Less: Closing stock of product M	2,000	2,025
Cost of sales	10,000	10,125
Less: NRV of by-product B		150
Net cost of sales		9,975
Gross profit		5,025

Notes

1 In (a) the closing stock of product M is valued as £12,000/12,000 units, i.e., £1 per unit, whereas in (b) the closing stock of product M is valued as £12,150/12,000 units, i.e., £1.0125 per unit. The slightly greater valuation of closing stock in (b) results in a slightly higher gross profit figure.

2 If the example included administration or selling costs relating to the major product, these would be deducted from the gross profit in order to arrive at a net profit.

Chapter 6

Joint Product Examples

Example 22

BKChemicals produces three joint products in one common process but each product is capable of being further processed separately after the split-off point. The estimated data given below relate to June:

	Product B	*Product K*	*Product C*
Selling price at split-off point (per litre)	£6	£8	£9
Selling price after further processing (per litre)	£10	£20	£30
Post-separation point costs	£20,000	£10,000	£22,500
Output in litres	3,500	2,500	2,000

Pre-separation point joint costs are estimated to be £40,000 and it is current practice to apportion these to the three products according to litres produced.

(a) You are required
  (i) to prepare a statement of estimated profit or loss for each product and in total for June if all three products are processed further, and
  (ii) to advise how profits could be maximised if one or more products are sold at the split-off point. Your advice should be supported by a profit statement. *11 marks*

(b) It has been suggested that responsibility accounting would be more relevant in BK Chemicals with the process incurring the common cost being treated as a profit centre.
  You are required
  (i) to explain briefly how this could best be achieved,
  (ii) to state the resulting profit to be shown for the common process, and
  (iii) to state two advantages of this approach. *5 marks*

(c) Discuss the problems associated with joint cost apportionments in relation to
(i) planning,
(ii) control, and
(iii) decision making.

9 marks

Total marks = 30

(a) (i) profit/loss if all three products are processed further

Apportionment of joint costs

Product	*Litres produced*	*Weighting*	*Joint costs apportioned* £
B	3,500	$^{35}/_{80} \times$ £40,000	17,500
K	2,500	$^{25}/_{80} \times$ £40,000	12,500
C	2,000	$^{20}/_{80} \times$ £40,000	10,000
	8,000		40,000

Profit/loss statement

	Product B		*Product K*		*Product C*		*Total*	
	£	£	£	£	£	£	£	£
Sales revenue		35,000		50,000		60,000		145,000
Joint costs apportioned	17,500		12,500		10,000		40,000	
Post-separation costs point	20,000		10,000		22,500		52,500	
		37,500		22,500		32,500		92,500
Profit (loss)		(2,500)		27,500		27,500		52,500

(ii) sale of the products at the split off point

Additional costs and revenues from further processing

	Product B	*Product K*	*Product C*
	£	£	£
Additional revenue	£4 × 3,500	£12 × 2,500	£21 × 2,000
	14,000	30,000	42,000
Additional costs	20,000	10,000	22,500
Additional profit(loss)	(6,000)	20,000	19,500

The firm will benefit if Product B is sold at the split-off point, and if Products K and C are processed further.

Profit statement

	Product B		Product K		Product C		Total	
	£	£	£	£	£	£	£	£
Sales revenue		21,000		50,000		60,000		131,000
Joint costs apportioned	17,500		12,500		10,000		40,000	
Post-separation point costs	–		10,000		22,500		32,500	
		17,500		22,500		32,500		72,500
Profit		3,500		27,500		27,500		58,500

This proves that the total profit increases by £6,000 if Product B is sold at the split-off point rather than being processed further.

(b) (i) If the process incurring the common cost is treated as a profit centre, then it must also receive revenues as well as incurring costs. The products will be transferred to the departments involved in further processing at a transfer price. This could be based on cost, but as there is a selling price for each product at the split-off point, it would seem sensible to use this as the transfer price.

(ii) The resulting profit for the common process would be the revenues at the split-off point, less the common costs.

		£
Revenues	Product B (3,500 × £6)	21,000
	Product K (2,500 × £8)	20,000
	Product C (2,000 × £9)	18,000
		59,000
Common costs		40,000
Profit		19,000

(iii) If the products were transferred out at a known price, then any increase in efficiency or reduction in costs would directly increase the profit of the responsibility centre.

If rewards or bonuses were paid to staff based on the reported profits, this could increase motivation and efficiency, possibly increasing profits further.

The use of transfer prices based on selling prices gives a much more accurate measure of the economic benefit of this part of the process.

NB: Only two advantages are required.

(c) (i) Joint costs can be apportioned in a number of different ways, the most common methods being based on the physical measure of output or on a measure of sales value. This is perfectly acceptable if the resulting data is used for stock valuation for profit determination. However, as there are a number of different ways of apportioning joint costs, each of which will result in a different measure of profit, care must be exercised if this data is used for any other purpose. Provided the user understands exactly how the data has been prepared and the assumptions underlying it, there is no danger, but a statement showing the apportionment of joint costs is of little use for planning purposes.

(ii) Control is normally achieved by comparing actual results with budgeted results, usually adjusted to reflect the actual level of output. The process of control normally assumes that the costs under consideration can be influenced by a responsible manager. If the costs under consideration have been apportioned to products, there is little that a manager can do to influence the costs attributed to each product. However, it is possible to influence and therefore control the total costs of the process, before they are apportioned to individual products. Any problems of controlling the costs attributed to specific products will be further compounded by the inclusion of both fixed and variable costs in the apportionment process.

(iii) Decisions should never be based on data containing cost apportionments, as different methods of cost apportionment could result in different decisions. If the decision is concerned with further processing, it is best simply to determine the contribution which will arise after deducting the additional processing costs from the additional revenue as a result of further processing. If the decision concerns the process itself, it should be remembered that in most cases the products arise jointly from a common process. If it is not possible to cease production of one or more of the products, then to stop selling one of the products will simply result in a loss of revenue.

Example 23

A company manufactures four products from an input of a raw material to process 1. Following this process, product A is processed in process 2, product B in process 3, product C in process 4 and product D in process 5.

The normal loss in process 1 is 10% of input, and there are no expected losses in the other processes. Scrap value in process 1 is £0.50 per litre. The costs incurred in process 1 are apportioned to each product according to the volume of output of each product. Production overhead is absorbed as a percentage of direct wages.

Data in respect of the month of October

	Process					
	1	*2*	*3*	*4*	*5*	*Total*
	£000	*£000*	*£000*	*£000*	*£000*	*£000*
Direct materials at £1.25 per litre	100					100
Direct wages	48	12	8	4	16	88
Production overhead						66

	Product			
	A	*B*	*C*	*D*
	litres	*litres*	*litres*	*litres*
Output	22,000	20,000	10,000	18,000
	£	£	£	£
Selling price	4.00	3.00	2.00	5.00
Estimated sales value at end of process 1	2.50	2.80	1.20	3.00

You are required to:

(a) Calculate the profit or loss for each product for the month, assuming all output is sold at the normal selling price. *8 marks*

(b) Suggest and evaluate an alternative production strategy which would optimise profit for the month. It should not be assumed that the output of process 1 can be changed. *5 marks*

(c) Suggest to what management should devote its attention, if it is to achieve the potential benefit indicated in (b). *3 marks*

Total marks = 16

Answer and explanation

(a) Calculate the profit or loss for each product for the month, assuming all output is sold at the normal selling price:

Process 1 account

	Litres	£000		Litres	CPU	£000
Materials	80,000	100	Normal loss	8,000	£0.50	4
Direct wages		48	Output (note 3)	70,000	£2.50	175
Production overhead absorbed (note 2)		36	Abnormal loss	2,000	£2.50	5
	80,000	184		80,000		184

Notes

1 It is necessary to determine the cost per litre for use in part (a).

2 The production overhead absorption rate is 75% of direct wages.

3 The 2,000 litres which are not accounted for as inputs into the subsequent processes must be considered as an abnormal loss.

4 The cost per litre is based on everything that is normal, i.e.

$$\frac{£184{,}000 - £4{,}000}{72{,}000 \text{ litres}} = £2.50 \text{ per litre}$$

Statement of profit (loss) for each product

	A	B	C	D	Total
	£000	£000	£000	£000	£000
Sales	88	60	20	90	258
Costs:					
Process 1 (£2.50 per litre)	55	50	25	45	175
Direct wages	12	8	4	16	40
Production overhead	9	6	3	12	30
	76	64	32	73	245
Profit (loss)	12	(4)	(12)	17	13

(b) An alternative production strategy which would optimise profit for the month: it should be determined whether the company is better off as a result of the further processing of the four products. This can be achieved by using the incremental approach and comparing the additional revenue from further processing with the additional costs.

	A	*B*	*C*	*D*	*Total*
	£000	*£000*	*£000*	*£000*	*£000*
Sales value after processing	88	60	20	90	258
Sales value at split-off point	55	56	12	54	177
Increase in sales value	33	4	8	36	81
Additional costs	21	14	7	28	70
Additional profit (loss)	12	(10)	1	8	11

The best production strategy would be to process products A, C and D through processes 2, 4 and 5 respectively, but to sell product B at the split-off point, as follows:

	A	*B*	*C*	*D*	*Total*
	£000	*£000*	*£000*	*£000*	*£000*
Sales	88	56	20	90	254
Additional costs	21	–	7	28	56
Contribution to Process 1	67	56	13	62	198
Process 1 costs					175
Overall profit					23

Note that this analysis assumes that all direct wages and production overheads are incremental costs if production is undertaken, and avoidable costs if production is not undertaken.

(c) Product B should not be processed through process 3, but should be sold at the split-off point.

Without the further processing of products A, C and D, process 1 on its own is only just profitable. The total revenue from 70,000 litres at the end of this process in October would be £177,000, with the normal costs for 70,000 litres of £175,000. The company should investigate such matters as the possibility of reducing costs or of increasing selling prices.

The methods of cost apportionment might also be further investigated, e.g., the effect of using the sales value method in apportioning the cost of process 1.

Example 24

Zeta Ltd operates a chemical process which jointly produces four products, A,B,C and D. All the products are sold without further processing.

Data for production and sales are as follows:

Produce	*Production* kg	*Sales* kg	*Selling price* per kg
			£
A	150,000	140,000	0.70
B	110,000	95,000	0.60
C	60,000	55,000	0.60
D	180,000	180,000	1.35

There were no opening stocks of any of the products. Closing stocks were ready for sale. The production costs of the process were £180,000.

(a) You are required to prepare profit statements, apportioning the joint costs using:

(i) the physical measures basis

(ii) the sales value basis *10 marks*

(b) Assume that products A, C and D have to undergo further processing before they can be sold. The data relating to this process is as follows:

Product	*Processing costs* per kg	*Final selling price* per kg
	£	£
A	0.50	1.70
C	0.20	1.20
D	0.12	1.42

You are required to prepare a revised profit statement apportioning the joint costs for all the products, using the net realisable (notional) sales value method. Assume the same level of production and sales as in (a).

6 marks

(c) Assume now that the firm has a choice. It can either sell products A, B, C and D at the split-off point, or it can undertake further processing on Products A, C and D. Show the additional profit or loss as a result of further processing and prepare a statement showing the total profit which will result from the optimal strategy. Assume that all the production can be sold.

6 marks

Total marks = 22

(a) (i) *Physical measures basis*

Apportionment of joint costs

Product	*Production*	*Weighting*	*Joint costs apportioned*	*Cost per unit*
	kg		£	£
A	150,000	$^{150}/_{500} \times$ £180,000	54,000	0.36
B	110,000	$^{110}/_{500} \times$ £180,000	39,600	0.36
C	60,000	$^{60}/_{500} \times$ £180,000	21,600	0.36
D	180,000	$^{180}/_{500} \times$ £180,000	64,800	0.36
	500,000		180,000	

Profit statement

	A		*B*		*C*		*D*		*Total*	
	£	£	£	£	£	£	£	£	£	£
Sales revenue		98,000		57,000		33,000		243,000		431,000
Joint costs										
apportioned	54,000		39,600		21,600		64,800		180,000	
Less: stock	3,600		5,400		1,800		—		10,800	
Cost of sales		50,400		34,200		19,800		64,800		169,200
Profit		47,600		22,800		13,200		178,200		261,800

(ii) *Sales value basis*

Apportionment of joint costs

Product	*Sales value*	*Weighting*	*Joint costs apportioned*	*Cost per unit*
	£		£	£
A	105,000	$^{105}/_{450} \times$ £180,000	42,000	0.28
B	66,000	$^{66}/_{450} \times$ £180,000	26,400	0.24
C	36,000	$^{36}/_{450} \times$ £180,000	14,400	0.24
D	243,000	$^{243}/_{450} \times$ £180,000	97,200	0.54
	450,000		180,000	

Profit statement

	A		B		C		D		Total	
	£	£	£	£	£	£	£	£	£	£
Sales revenue		98,000		57,000		33,000		243,000		431,000
Joint costs apportioned	42,000		26,400		14,400		97,200		180,000	
Less: stock	2,800		3,600		1,200		—		7,600	
Cost of sales		39,200		22,800		13,200		97,200		172,400
Profit		58,800		34,200		19,800		145,800		258,600

Notes

1 When apportioning the joint costs using the sales value basis, the *sales value of production* must be used, not the sales revenue

2 The cost per unit is the same for each product when apportioning the joint costs using the physical measures basis and the gross profit ratio (at 60%) is the same when using the sales value basis.

(b) *Net realisable (notional) sales value basis*

Apportionment of joint costs

Product	*Final sales value*	*Additional processing costs*	*Net realisable (notional) sales value*	*Weighting*	*Joint costs apportioned*	*Cost per unit*
	£	£	£		£	£
A	255,000	75,000	180,000	$^{180}/_{540} \times$ £180,000	60,000	0.4+0.5
B	66,000	–	66,000	$^{66}/_{540} \times$ £180,000	22,000	0.2
C	72,000	12,000	60,000	$^{60}/_{540} \times$ £180,000	20,000	0.33+0.2
D	255,600	21,600	234,000	$^{234}/_{540} \times$ £180,000	78,000	not needed
	648,600	108,600	540,000		180,000	

Profit/loss statement

	A		B		C		D		Total	
	£	£	£	£	£	£	£	£	£	£
Sales revenue		238,000		57,000		66,000		255,600		616,600
Joint costs apportioned	60,000		22,000		20,000		78,000		180,000	
Additional costs	75,000		–		12,000		21,600		108,000	
	135,000		22,000		32,000		99,600		288,600	
Less: stock	9,000		3,000		2,650		–		14,650	
Cost of sales		126,000		19,000		29,350		99,600		273,950
Gross profit		112,000		38,000		36,650		156,000		342,650

(c) *Further processing decision*

	A	C	D
Addition revenue	£1 × 150,000	£0.60 × 110,000	£0.07 × 180,000
	150,000	66,000	12,600
Additional costs	75,000	12,000	21,600
Additional profit (loss)	£75,000	£54,000	£ (9,000)

Optimal strategy

	A	B	C	D	Total	
	£	£	£	£	£	£
Sales at split-off point		66,000				66,000
Sales after processing	255,000		72,000	255,600		582,600
Total revenue	255,000	66,000	72,000	255,600		648,600
Joint costs					180,000	
Additional costs	75,000	—	12,000	21,600	108,600	
Total costs						288,600
Total profit						360,000

It is not necessary to apportion the joint costs because there is no stock to be valued as it is assumed that all the production can be sold.